Cleansing
&
Healing Streams

By

Dr. Shirley Christian

Cleansing and Healing Streams
Copyright © January 2003
Shirley Christian Ministries
In Streams of His Grace
ISBN 978-0-6151-6271-3

www.shirleychristian.org

Table of Contents

HEALING IS THE CHILDREN'S BREAD

"It is not good to take the children's bread and throw it to the dogs." But she said, "Yes, Lord; but even the dogs feed on the crumbs which fall from their masters' table." Then Jesus said to her, "O woman, your faith is great; it shall be done for you as you wish." And her daughter was healed at once. (Matthew 15:26-28)

To an unbeliever, a Canaanite, Jesus spoke these words that initially seem harsh from our loving Savior. They were relevant to those who fear God—His children, and those who do not—who are outside covenant. Similarly, Jesus said to a Samaritan woman who was also outside the covenant:

"You worship what you do not know; we worship what we know, for salvation is from the Jews." (John 4:22)

The Canaanite woman called Jesus "Master," and He rewarded her faith by demonstrating that He is the Healer and Deliverer. Her daughter experienced cleansing and healing streams of the Master. He called this woman's persevering faith "great."

The Samaritan woman of John 4 had married five men, and was living with a man who was not her husband. She came to understand that God provided Jesus the Christ as Salvation—which also could bring about her emotional healing. He had living water for her.

Those who fear God enjoy salvation through the blood of the Eternal Covenant—the very blood of Christ. For them, salvation is free, healing is the Children's bread, and through Christ, God provides many streams of cleansing and healing. You also may enter these streams now.

They didn't thirst when he led them through the deserts; he caused the waters to flow out of the rock for them; he split the rock also, and the waters gushed out. (Isaiah 48:21)

INTRODUCTION

Something was missing or broken. Unhappiness was the norm for me. I constantly felt defeated. My muscles ached, my joints felt stiff, I did not sleep well, and I had migraine headaches every weekend. Yes, every weekend. Medication dulled some of the symptoms, but the roots remained. Doctors can prescribe pills that will numb the emotions, but feeling neither excited nor depressed is not the answer! I learned to handle unhappiness and symptoms of depression by focusing on other things and by doing what I could to combat stress. Like the majority, I often looked to obtain what was missing in the wrong ways.

Brokenness can easily go unnoticed with one becomes a workaholic. While we suffer because of it, we often fail to realize that we apply ourselves to such an extent out of a sense of rejection and a need for approval, both within and without. As have many in such situations, I had heard and read the Bible, but it lacked power for me. Sure, our mainstream denominational churches (thank God for them) taught about grace and forgiveness, but I learned little about the empowerment grace provides to overcome sin and its effects. Such teachings fall on deaf ears when an obstacle exists. Overall, the Bible read to me more like a history book about something that happened to a unique people. The churches I attended seemed to avoid focusing on the Holy Spirit and the power of the Word that is available to believers. We had blinders!

Through a supernatural encounter with the Lord, my life changed. I began to believe the Bible! Subsequently, the Holy Spirit led me to a book that showed me that that men and women of our day had walked and demonstrated the power of its promises. This book about John G. Lake forever made an impact on me. I got angry. If John G. Lake was able to walk in such power, fulfillment, and experience God so remarkably, why was I not doing so, and why had no one told me that I could? Clearly, the first and even several generations later of Jesus' followers flowed in this power—the

Scriptures show us that some, who were not eye witnesses of Jesus' earthly ministry, appropriated the power of the gospel. Paul, a Jewish believer, saw Jesus in a vision, and tells us,

> Truly the signs of the apostle were worked out among you in all patience, in miracles and in wonders, and by works of power. (2 Corinthians 12:12 MKJV)

I threw away the prescriptions, the backward religious mindset, and I began a journey, a quest, to study the Bible with a new emphasis toward laying hold of the promises it contained, and a special emphasis on healing and wholeness, since I needed it so greatly. I developed a desire to truly know the God of the Bible and His dear Son. I fasted frequently, both of short and long durations, prayed fervently, studied greatly, and believed God big-time. Years later, I began ministering in Healing School in our local church. I taught and ministered to the sick during the week for over seven years. During that time, God performed healings, miracles and deliverance through me. While I do not claim to have captured all of what is to be known about healing, God has revealed much to me, along with what I gleaned from others such as John G. Lake, Smith Wigglesworth, Kenneth E. Hagin, and many other pioneers of the Healing Revival. Jesus Christ, of course, it the foremost example for all time.

If John G. Lake was able to walk in such power, fulfillment, and experience God so remarkably, why was I not doing so, and why had no one told me that I could?

My goal is to impart some of the things that I have learned about God and divine healing, and some experiences to encourage all to believe God. Yes, like a little child, believe the Bible and in doing so, believe God. Jesus warns,

> Most certainly I tell you, whoever will not receive the Kingdom of God like a little child, he will in no way enter into it. (Mark 10:15)

The Kingdom awaits such as you.

ENTERING CLEANSING AND HEALING STREAMS

I have used the term "Cleansing and Healing Streams" to describe the various streams of divine healing that the Bible shows are available to us. While healing may manifest naturally as an outflow of the way in which God made us, through doctors, or by Divine means, it all stems from God, our Source, and is an outflow of His merciful, compassionate and gracious nature. Being gracious means that God has a nature of goodness, and to be compassionate is to be full of tender mercies.

The word "salvation" encompasses the healing that so many need in this life. One can be saved, made whole, healed—all made available to us by our reconciliation with God through Christ Jesus. We have may have failed to appropriate healing as we should, but it is available nonetheless.

God prescribed a number of different streams from which one can experience His cleansing, delivering and healing power. We see that healing is greatly needed today by so many in the world. Surely, it must grieve the Lord Jesus to see those of His body, the church, beset with disease and pain when He died for the Church's glory. In every pew or chair across America, children of God sit with something they should no longer continue to tolerate. Whether the reason for healing is for damaged emotions, physical ailments, or for spiritual or mental areas, wholeness is available for all. God desires His family to be well. Yes, even cancers and terminal diseases have a remedy through the Good News of the Kingdom of God through Jesus Christ. Whatever the ailment, the Healer is alive, and has given His body many different streams of healing for divine health.

E.W. Kenyon first wrote of "methods" for receiving healing in his book, Jesus the Healer. He speaks of five methods through which healings are obtained.[1] While making use of the methods discussed in his writing, I have also focused on other areas by which God heals; for example, through praise and worship, deliverance and angelic activity.

---

[1] *E.W, Kenyon "Jesus the Healer"* 36-38

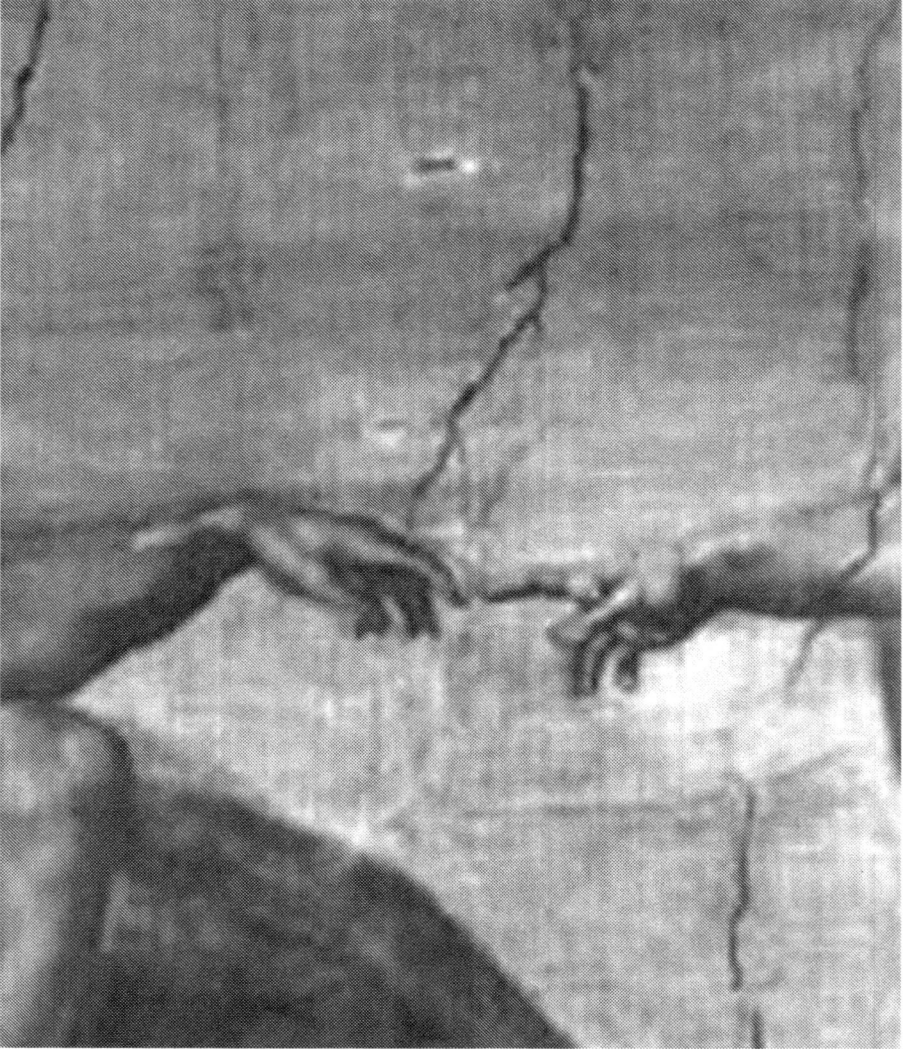

They didn't thirst when he led them through the deserts; he caused the waters to flow out of the rock for them; he split the rock also, and the waters gushed out. (Isaiah 48:21)

CHAPTER ONE

WHAT IS DIVINE HEALING?

"Divine healing" is a term used to describe supernatural healing. A definition for divine healing can be broken down as follows: Divine is relating to or characteristic of God, the transcendent omnipresent, omnipotent, omniscient God. Healing means renewal or regeneration or restoration of a person from a weak or diseased state. You might think of it as a recovery process that ultimately results in wholeness, either soundness or physical, mental or spiritual health. God's spiritual, physical, and mental laws must be internalized and externalized. It can mean harmony within and without. People may have sickness and disease not only from outright oppression, but also from unresolved inner issues (for example—guilt or unforgiveness), or any rebellion to God's ways. For many, healing may need to focus on obedience, repentance, forgiveness and overcoming unbelief.

Physical pain and disease have a remedy in Christ Jesus. Jesus demonstrated God's compassionate nature toward sickness and disease during His earthly ministry. Your job is to learn to receive whatever appropriate remedy the condition may require.

Some sicknesses do not have a spiritual root, but come as a result of the curse. However, many times sickness and disease have a root other than the natural fallen state of today's world.

The Sin and Sickness Connection

And behold, they were bringing to Him a paralytic, lying on a bed; and Jesus seeing their faith said to the paralytic, "Take courage, My son, your sins are forgiven." And behold, some of the scribes said to themselves, "This fellow blasphemes." And Jesus knowing their thoughts said, "Why are you thinking evil in your hearts? "For which is easier, to say, 'Your sins are forgiven,' or to say, 'Rise, and walk'? "But in order that you may know that the Son of Man has authority on earth to forgive sins"-- then He said to the

11

paralytic-- "Rise, take up your bed, and go home" (Matthew 9:2-6).

Jesus does not make a distinction between the sickness and the cause of the sickness—its root, which is sin. His future sacrifice would take place for both sin and sickness. Jesus repeats this reference to sin and sickness in a subsequent verse where the Pharisees deride him for eating with sinners. He again uses the analogy of sickness to sin.

> And when the Pharisees saw this, they said to His disciples, "Why is your Teacher eating with the tax-gatherers and sinners?" But when He heard this, He said, 'It is not those who are healthy who need a physician, but those who are sick'" (Matthew 9:11-12).

Many, like the leper who came to Jesus, believe God can heal them, but they are unsure if He wants to heal them. Jesus says, "I am willing." This is the same Jesus who is "the same yesterday and today, yes and forever" (see Hebrews 13:8). He has not changed and is not willing to see any go away with sickness. His will is clear. "Who desires all men to be saved and to come to the knowledge of the truth" (1Timothy 2:4). Not all will be saved—made whole, but His will is that all be saved. His will is for all to be healed because he redeemed us from sickness. We have a perfect redemption in Jesus. Just as we are made righteous His faith, inheriting eternal life, we are healed by faith.

Jesus also used leaven to make an analogy to sin. "Be on your guard against the leaven (ferment) of the Pharisees, which is hypocrisy (producing unrest and violent agitation)" (Luke 12:1 AMP). Recall also at the Passover, the Israelites were commanded to remove all leaven from their households, a type of repentance, a putting away of sin. Hypocrisy is sin. It is pretending, when in reality the hypocrite's heart is far from God. Jesus explains, "These people honor me with their lips; but their heart is far from me" (Matthew 15:8).

The Apostle Paul uses a similar analogy of leaven symbolizing sin. He commands the Corinthian church to be done with tolerating sin in their midst.

Do you not know that a little leaven will ferment the whole lump (of dough). Purge (clean out) the old leaven that you may be fresh (new) dough, still uncontaminated (as you are), for Christ, our Passover (Lamb), has been sacrificed. Therefore, let us keep the feast, not with old leaven, not with leaven of vice and malice and wickedness, but with the unleavened (bread) of purity (nobility, honor) and sincerity and (unadulterated) truth (1 Corinthians 5:6-8 AMP).

Many references in the Bible show us that sin and sickness are spoken of in the same breath. Notice the elements of the propitiation in the following verses: forgiveness, healing, deliverance, safety, prosperity and long life.

Bless the LORD, O my soul, and forget none of His benefits; Who pardons all your iniquities; who heals all your diseases; Who redeems your life from the pit; who crowns you with lovingkindness and compassion; Who satisfies your years with good things, so that your youth is renewed like the eagle (Psalm 103:2-5).

In the fifth chapter of James, Christians are told what to do under certain circumstances if they are sick. The weak one, who because of weakness cannot come to the church, must call for help.

Is anyone among you sick? Let him call for the elders of the church, and let them pray over him, anointing him with oil in the name of the Lord; and the prayer offered in faith will restore the one who is sick, and the Lord will raise him up, and if he has committed sins, they will be forgiven him (James 5:14-15).

Notice this passage says the prayer in faith will restore the sick one, and if he has sins, they will be forgiven him. Again, we see the how the Bible, the inspired Word of God, treats sin and sickness. It is because the two are inseparable.

God wants His body healed. Loving us to the degree that He does, I suggest that He wants us to be healed even more than we want to be healed! After all, He sent His Son to us. Both sickness and sin were dealt with at the cross.

CLEANSING AND HEALING STREAMS FOR EMOTIONAL SICKNESS

I believe spiritual issues lie at the root of many diseases. People that experience some sort of rejection or separation issues suffer from anxiety disorders of many different kinds. They do not feel close to God, and feeling unloved by God—are at odds with Him, and with His Word. A sense of enmity prevails in their relationships as well. That means they are feeling separation with God, themselves and others.

> *The one who does not accept his or herself feels internal separation, and does not love him or herself, and may know condemnation, guilt, and self-hatred.*

This is what happened in the Garden of Eden involving the curse. Man experienced disharmony with God, himself, others, and creation. All this occurred as a result of sin and the resulting spiritual death—which is separation from God. Any sense of separation from God results in separation in other areas. Satan deceived Eve into believing that she lacked something that would make her more like God, apart from God—she was already like God—made in His image and likeness. She sought to fill this perceived lack with something God had forbidden.

The one who does not accept his or herself feels internal separation, and does not love his or herself, and may know a measure of condemnation, shame, guilt, and self-hatred. The same is true of this person's relationships with others. They may be haunted by jealousy, hatred, bitterness and a sense of being unloved.

Soul sickness is as real as the physical sickness it may produce. It is a great sickness that eats away at a person until possibly, it even turns to cancer or some other disease. Rebellious cells go to work within a person's body. Different types of fear are also a major basis for many autoimmune diseases. Fear of judgment comes with condemnation and amounts to a fear of facing Christ at His judgment

14

seat. How could you fear the One who died for you? Peterson paraphrases,

> And who would dare tangle with God by messing with one of God's chosen? Who would dare even to point a finger? The One who died for us—who was raised to life for us!—is in the presence of God at this very moment sticking up for us. (Romans 8:33-34 MSG)

When an emotional pain grips you, it hurts as much as a physical pain. In fact, it is just as important that you be healed of emotional pain or you will most likely have physical pain develop.

Some are suffering because they never learned to avoid the pain of offense. Jesus said that it is impossible for offenses to not come (Matthew 18:17). It seems to be a part of life. Offense is the Greek word *skandalon*. It may be described as a trap or cause of stumbling (Strong 4625). An offense has to be received to be effective. I think of it as accepting the devil's fiery darts when you allow an offense to affect you. You must determine that words or actions cannot harm you unless you allow them to become an offense. They are only as significant as you allow. Apply yourself to the Word of God and maintain healing. You must also guard against causing offense. Avoid judging and forming opinions, and make allowances for other people. Had you rather judge and form an opinion or be healthy?

Wounds to the heart are as painful and often more devastating than physical wounds. Living with a parent or spouse who abuses you verbally and withholds love unless you do something to earn it can be just as devastating to your heart as physical abuse—maybe more so. Abuse has many faces. It may seem unmanly or cowardly for a man to pound a spouse or loved one with his fists (even though some do), but it is just as evil to pound someone with words. Words are

Wounds to the heart are as painful and often more devastating than physical wounds.

powerful, and if they are evil and harsh, they leave bruises and deep wounds beneath the surface—but wounds nonetheless. The Bible says, "Thoughtless words can wound as deeply as any sword, but wisely spoken words can heal" (Proverbs 12:18 GNB).

Women are especially vulnerable to internalizing anger from abuse. They call it being hurt. When someone is hurt, they are usually not able to express anger. Maybe they were raised not to show emotions, or learned to get attention from withdrawing to draw out sympathy from others. It is basically anger.

A spirit of rejection is frequently accompanied by internalized anger. Something or someone failed to show this person acceptance and love at a young age or failed to cover them, and it caused them to become vulnerable to a spirit of rejection. It produces a sense of brokenness, the feeling of being an outcast in one's own family. Wisdom says, "The spirit of a man will sustain his infirmity; but a broken spirit who can bear?" (Proverbs 18:14).

When my mind or heart is wounded, it makes for a dirty wound. If healing is not sought through forgiveness and repentance, then I not only have my own wound fester, I may begin to wound others. The abused becomes the abuser. It has been said, "Hurting people hurt people." Like infection in the body, a wound in your soul will infect others—just like infection spreads in a physical sense.

Often we need to seek the power in the Word to provide cleansing from more than contamination from sin, but for painful wounds experienced because we live in a fallen world. Sorrow, pain and suffering are common to people at some time. Some wounds are clean. They will heal unless something causes infection. If guilt, shame, self-pity, or bitterness comes in, the wound becomes deep and festers. Shame comes from being wounded by others. Guilt is often from our own failings—self-inflicted wounds. It comes from violating our own sense of right and wrong. Time does not heal these type wounds—if it did, then we would not need the Lord.

Restoration from Emotionally Based Sickness

If you have known the feeling of uncontrollable anger, internalized anger, or the pain of rejection and the sense of being an outcast, an orphan at heart, then I have good news for you. Jesus came to bind up the broken hearted (see Isaiah 61:1). Your heart can have peace and experience freedom from tormenting spirits. God prophesied that He would restore the outcast, and heal them. "For I will restore you to health, and I will heal your wounds, says the Lord;

16

because they have called you an outcast . . . " (Jeremiah 30:17). You can believe your God loves you and will take your mourning and give you a garland instead. Isaiah prophesied,

> To care for the needs of all who mourn in Zion, give them bouquets of roses instead of ashes, Messages of joy instead of news of doom, a praising heart instead of a languid spirit. Rename them "Oaks of Righteousness" planted by GOD to display his glory. (Isaiah 61:3 MSG)

Healing is not just for my physical body, but also for my whole person. My mind and heart need restoration by the Great Physician. I must have peace within to have peace without. This is the meaning of being saved—made whole.

Much of the sickness and disease people experience comes not only from guilt, self-condemnation, and fear, but unforgiveness. Unforgiveness is sometimes rooted in those who cannot seem to forgive themselves. They do not understand the value that God placed on the blood of Jesus. Pride refuses to believe the value God placed on the blood of Christ as the satisfaction for all sin. If you have fallen into this trap, then hear this: Christ Jesus' blood satisfied God. He loved the world so much that He sent His Son to die as the atoning sacrifice (see John 3:16). The blood of Christ Jesus satisfied all the claims of justice, and silenced the devil's

Unforgiveness is sometimes rooted in those who cannot seem to forgive themselves.

accusations against you, and any accusations he might bring against God's justice for pardoning you. Now it is up to you to receive what He has done, accept the value God placed on the blood, and let go of condemnation, guilt, fear, and unforgiveness of others and yourself. Jesus said,

> And whenever you stand praying, if you have anything against anyone, forgive him and let it drop (leave it, let it go), in order that your Father Who is in heaven may also forgive you your [own] failings and shortcomings and let them drop. (Mark 11:25 AMP).

17

Allow me to emphasize this: "Let it go, and let it drop." This applies to forgiving yourself as well as others. If not, you will live in a state of guilt and expectation of punishment. Your own soul will comply with your belief. While I am not under the law, the Bible indicates that I can develop a law within myself, my conscience bearing witness to it, and my mind accusing me or excusing me (see Romans 2:15). If I do not have peace within myself, then my mind accuses me, and something will be out of kilter. It will cause unease and a guilty conscience. The value of a conscience free of condemnation is highly underrated. The Apostle Paul often spoke of keeping a clear conscience (see Acts 24:16, Romans 13:5). We must live out of our hearts for conscience sake. A person at rest in spirit, soul, and body with God is a whole, healed person.

After King David sinned by taking Bathsheba, the wife of Uriah, and murdering him to cover his sin, Nathan the Prophet confronted him (2 Samuel 11). The guilt became an overwhelming burden to him. In Psalm 51, he pours out his grief and desire for fellowship with God to be restored. God forgave David. The wonderful part of this story is how David received God's forgiveness. It revived him.

We must learn to receive forgiveness as easily. The spirit and soul are intertwined in the heart. Notice the difference in the following Bible versions. "He restores my soul" (Psalm 23:3). "He restores my spirit" (Psalm 23:3 NJB). Just as the Word of God came to David through the prophet, the Word of God kept before us will continue to reveal the condition of our hearts. When we repent and seek forgiveness, God will cleanse us from unrighteousness to affect healing and fellowship (see 1 John 1:9).

Looking within yourself leads to trying to be approved and accepted by God and man for who you are—not who Christ is in you and what He did on your behalf. Without realizing it, you seek to live under the law (dead works), and if you are under law, then you are not under grace (Romans 4:14). You will not be empowered by the grace from faith's uprightness. You cannot experience true peace if you strive to be approved and accepted. You already are in Christ. He qualified you for all the blessings—your inheritance (Colossians 1:2).

I believe people can stop any self-loathing and fear because of sin and failures by recognizing who Christ is in them. As we behold Him, we are changed (see 2 Corinthians 3:18). It requires ceasing to look to one's self for perfection, and looking to the righteousness we partake of in Christ through the cross. So many who live under condemnation and guilt from sin, need to come to Christ, and begin to grow in the knowledge of His completed work.

Cling to who you are in union with Him, totally upright and holy. Realize that anything that accuses or condemns you is not of God—He sees you in union with Christ. God loves you as much as He loves Jesus (see John 17:26). When you unite yourself to Christ, you are one spirit with Him (see 1 Corinthians 6:17). No more is it just you, it is Christ in you, hope of glory (see Colossians 1:27). This does not mean you are exempt from fulfilling the moral requirements Jesus commanded, but rather that you are empowered to do so by His grace. You have been forgiven for past sins, will be cleansed from current sins, and justified into the future. Paul explains,

> God made this sinless man be a sin offering on our
> behalf, so that in union with Him we might fully share
> in God's righteousness. (2 Corinthians 5:21 JNT)

It took faith for you to believe—when you did, God acquitted you—justified you. Now use the empowerment you have from the grace you received by the faith of Jesus,, not your own works, to live out of your heart, out of who Christ is in you. Become on the outside what you already are on the inside. Become what you behold— literally, become what you believe.

The process ultimately begins with you forgiving those who you believe hurt you, including God, if you hold Him responsible. To the extent that you hate or blame your parents, your position, or your life, I submit to you that you probably hate God. He is the one who gave you your parents. You may have made wrong choices along the way that added to your pain, but you may ultimately hold God responsible. You may need to meditate on this. Forgiveness and mercy will result in extending forgiveness and mercy, and wholeness.

The remedy of much soul sicknesses and some physical sicknesses for some is found in three areas; understanding the great love that moved God to send His Son into the world, esteeming the value of the blood of Christ, and realizing that every sin is remitted when we receive Him as our Lord. Otherwise, we are rejecting God's love, and the benefits of the work of God through Christ. Your own heart will condemn you if you don't believe with your heart. A condemned heart awaits punishment. If you don't believe this, then you will be subject to expecting judgment and punishment. Fear will take root and manifest in sickness. Fear is a self-fulfilling prophecy.

If something is amiss in your soul area, your body, or a wound to your spirit, the Lord is within you to bring wholeness. The Psalmist declares, "You will perfect that which concerns me" (Psalm 138:8).

The Psalmist reached out to God when rejection threatened his peace. "My father and mother walked out and left me, but GOD took me in." (Psalm 27:10 MSG). Have confidence that while parents may protect for a time, the Lord is a refuge forever. Even if someone failed to "cover you" and look out for you, the Lord will. I can see that what others reject, the Lord takes in, and confounds the world with it. Each of us has gone through or will go through pain and sorrow in life. Our Lord experienced profound betrayal from one of His disciples, denial from another, and rejection and judgment from His own countrymen, and even His Father turning from Him when He became sin on the cross—all for us. He experienced shame when he hung naked on the cross—so we do not have to. If someone has done something to you that caused you to experience shame, the Lord is your Healer. If you have done something to someone that brings you guilt, the Lord is your Healer. He made healing from these things available.

Soundness of soul comes when you recognize and receive who God has made you to be in union with Him, and your soul lines up with this belief. You hold nothing back from Him, and realize because you are in Him in covenant that "All things belong to you" (1 Corinthians 3:21). This is found by trusting Him.

We are never healed or made to feel whole by trying to gain love or acceptance apart from the finished work of Christ. Healing

20

does not come by trying to satisfy an inner need outwardly. God must be first place in everything. John encourages,

> Little children, keep yourselves from idols (false gods)—[from anything and everything that would occupy the place in your heart due to God, from any sort of substitute for Him that would take first place in your life]. Amen (so let it be). (1 John 5:21 AMP)

Jesus accused the church in Ephesus of having lost their first love.

> But I have this [one charge to make] against you: that you have left (abandoned) the love that you had at first [you have deserted Me, your first love]. (Revelation 2:4)

I believe that wholeness is the end result of full understanding within your heart of all the benefits Christ died to give mankind, and the great love God bestows on us. It amounts to understanding who Christ is in you, and what you have. It includes experiencing God's love as you recognize His great gift to you, and receiving the fullness of His Spirit.. We must come to know the love of God in Christ. Let this verse become real to you:

> And we have come to know and to believe the love that God has for us. God is love, and the one who remains in love remains in God, and God remains in him. (1John 4:16 HCSB)

Love is the healing factor for all. It will help you let go of the past—your past is a stepping-stone to your future. As your roots go deep, you experience love deeply. It will help you shake off past hurts, and stop seeking love in wrong ways. As you see such love, it is easy to stop competing with others—God has a unique plan for you. Face up to whatever the problem is, and call it by name: rejection, fear, jealousy or shame—whatever, and get rid of their fruits such as unforgiveness, bitterness, rebellion or anger.

Your past is a stepping-stone to your future

Because righteousness and holiness are in Jesus, and you are in Him, you may partake of God's very righteousness and holiness. It is so important that you understand Christ is all-in-all. You are required to lay down self-efforts to be accepted by God and receive His free gift of uprightness and accept Christ as your substitute. God has blessed you with every spiritual blessing in the heavenly places in Christ (see Ephesians 1:3).

Christians should have such peace and confidence that worry or fear is a thing of the past. Peace is synonymous with wholeness in my vocabulary, and I believe in God's. I refer you to the Hebrew word for peace and well-being, *Shalom*—nothing missing and nothing broken. The effect of knowing righteousness and beginning to live it is peace and confidence.

> And the work of righteousness shall be peace; and the effect of righteousness, quietness and confidence forever. (Isaiah 32:7)

Paul explained to us his sense of confidence in God through Christ. "I know in whom I have believed and am persuaded that he is able to keep that which I have committed to him against that day" (2 Timothy 1:12).

When you know who Christ is in you, the power of grace through faith in Christ as your sin offering empowers you to live righteously. You find that you are healed from the inside out. You will have understood that the relationship you have with the Creator and His Son through the Holy Spirit means you have grace, the power so that you can and will align your life with His spiritual principles. This is wholeness.

Succinctly, restoration begins by receiving the peace with God that Jesus died to bring, and then bringing one's self into right standing with His Word, one's own self, others and creation. This is the harmony we lost at Eden, and which is restored in Christ.

If it is true that the roots of many diseases and mental disorders are found in unresolved spiritual issues, then spiritual restoration is the answer. In summary, **the first step** in being healed is finding out what God has to say, and then coming into harmony with Him, His Word, His ways, and His plan for you from eternity.

This means you must find harmony within yourself as well, and accept yourself as He sees you. Also, you must resolve issues in your relationships that are not in harmony with the Word.

The second step must be to let go of the past, and believe that you are accepted in Christ, and qualified for all of God's blessings through Him. You must experience love to give love. You must experience peace to live in peace and harmony with those around you. Whatever is lacking, you can find as you look to God. He will build and restore. He promised to restore the years that you experienced devastation (see Joel 2:25).

Foremost, believe that God will bring a redemptive purpose from all that someone did or failed to do to you

Foremost, believe that God will bring a redemptive purpose from all that was someone did or failed to do to you. He will perfect that which concerns you (see Psalm 138:8). Trust God. As you turn to Him, He will forgive and cleanse. Cleansing is for sins we currently need to repent from, and be sprinkled with the blood of Christ Jesus.

> The people chosen according to the foreknowledge of God the Father through the sanctifying work of the Spirit to be obedient to Jesus Christ and to be sprinkled with his blood. May grace and peace be yours in abundance! (1 Peter 1:2)

> If we confess our sins, he is faithful and righteous to forgive us those sins and cleanse us from all unrighteousness. (1 John 1:9)

Please take a moment and refer now to the last page of **CHAPTER TEN**, *Cleansing and Healing Stream* **10,** for a prayer of cleansing and healing. You may want to read the entire chapter before the prayer. It more fully explains how to be free from all oppression.

They didn't thirst when he led them through the deserts; he caused
the waters to flow out of the rock for them; he split the rock also,
and the waters gushed out. (Isaiah 48:21)

CHAPTER TWO

THE STARTING POINT-FAITH AND THE WILL OF GOD

The Bible reveals a history of God healing people supernaturally under the Old Covenant. It showed God's will for healing through God's redemptive nature—a revelation of His nature to heal. God is constant. God speaks through Malachi, "For I, the LORD do not change" (Malachi 3:6B). In Numbers, Moses writes,

> God is not a man that He should lie, nor a son of man
> that He should repent; Has He said, and will He not do
> it? Or has He spoken, and will He not make it good?"
> (Numbers 23:19)

Just a few examples from the Old Testament show us God's healing nature: When the Israelites were delivered from Egypt, not one was sick among them. "He brought them forth also with silver and gold: and there was not one feeble person among their tribes." (Psalm 105:37). At the waters of Marah, God demonstrates compassion and healing:

> And he cried unto the Lord; and the Lord shewed him a
> tree, which when he had cast into the waters, the waters
> were made sweet: there he made for them a statute and
> an ordinance, and there he proved them, And said, If
> thou wilt diligently hearken to the voice of the Lord thy
> God, and wilt do that which is right in His sight, and
> wilt give ear to His commandments, and keep all his
> statutes, I will put none of these diseases upon thee,
> which I have brought upon the Egyptians: for I am the
> Lord that healeth thee. (Exodus 15: 25, 26 KJV)

God is the Healer—His name is connected with healing. In the laws for conquest of the promised land, He said through Moses,

But you shall serve the Lord your God, and He will bless your bread and water; and I remove sickness from your midst . . . I will fulfill the number of your days. (Exodus 23:25-26)

Many scriptures show the promise of long life, of longevity—and a long life is an indication of a healthy life. Obedience is a factor. Writes Moses,

That your days may be multiplied, and the days of your children, in the land which the Lord sware unto your fathers to give them, as the days of heaven upon the earth. (Deuteronomy 11:9, 21 KJV)

The Psalms have a number of examples of healing promises. David sings, "Whenever we're sick and in bed, GOD becomes our nurse, nurses us back to health" (Psalm 41:3 MSG).

Under the New Covenant, Jesus and His disciples also healed people supernaturally after He commissioned them. Salvation, healing, prosperity, deliverance, and protection are all contained in the kingdom message Jesus preached and demonstrated (see Chapter 8).

At Pentecost, God poured out the Holy Spirit and the opportunity for us to be endued with power! He also provides gifts of the Spirit, which include healing gifts (see 1 Corinthians 12). Thus, in our dispensation, healing is still available.

In thirteen cases of sixteen healings observed in the gospels, Jesus referred to the person's faith as responsible for their healing. To the woman who had been plagued with a hemorrhage for twelve years, and who pressed in to touch the hem of His garment for healing, He said, "Your faith has made you whole" (Mark 5:34). This tells us that faith is a major issue in healing. In his classic work "Christ the Healer," F.F. Bosworth writes, "Faith begins where the will of God is known." Therefore, it is important what you believe about the will of God, and that you believe healing is available. Just as with many of today, the people of Jesus' own home town became offended and refused to believe in Him, even with all His mighty works. They failed to obtain what He was able and willing to give. Mark records:

Is this not the carpenter, the Son of Mary, and brother of James, Joses, Judas, and Simon? And are not His sisters here with us?" So they were offended at Him. But Jesus said to them, "A prophet is not without honor except in his own country, among his own relatives, and in his own house." Now He could do no mighty work there, except that He laid His hands on a few sick people and healed them. And He marveled because of their unbelief. Then He went about the villages in a circuit, teaching. (Mark 6: 3-6)

Unbelief will stop up the flow of God's work. It will frustrate His purposes and cause blessings to be held up. The Psalmist writes how Israel did just that—they put God to the test and limited what He could do for them: "Yes, again and again they tempted God, and limited the Holy One of Israel" (Psalm 78:41 KJV). Faith can have the opposite effect! Expectancy (confident expectation, which defines faith) and desire can be a catalyst for bringing God on the scene. The Chronicler exhorts:

For the eyes of the LORD run to and fro throughout the whole earth, to show Himself strong on behalf of those whose heart is loyal to Him. (2 Chronicles 16:9)

God is a faith-God. He looks to show Himself strong to those whose hearts are fully His. In the New Testament, Jesus said, "Nevertheless, when the Son of Man comes, will He really find faith on the earth?" (Luke 18:8). When a heart is fully His, it trusts. Faith (trust) must be important if we cannot please God without it, and Jesus is looking for it when He returns (see Hebrews 11:6).

Jesus said that He only did what He saw His Father doing and that He came to do God's will (see John 5:19, 6:38). Consequently, if He healed the sick, He was doing God's will. It follows that if He healed the sick according to God's will, then God must not be the one making people sick. Just the opposite.

Jesus Healed the Sick

We frequently picture Jesus as only laying His hands on people or speaking to a disease. Yet, sometimes, Jesus would ask the person wanting healing to do something unusual, requiring obedience as the person put action to their faith. An example is when Jesus said to the blind man, "Go, wash in the pool of Siloam" (John 9:7). Jesus often said that the person's faith brought the healing, but not in every instance.

The overall theme in the examples of healing in the gospels is that Jesus felt compassion for the sick person and healed them at their point of need. Whether they demonstrated "great faith" or simple "childlike faith," the Lord met them at their point of need and healed them. Similarly, he gave the disciples authority in His name to heal the sick, and He prayed for all who would believe in His name (Matthew 10, Luke 9, John 17:20 respectively).

In the Book of Acts, the apostles were not limited to one method of healing. Healing and authority in the name of Jesus did not go away with the last of the apostles—the Apostle Jesus Christ is still alive—He has risen and lives in us. Writes the author of Hebrews,

> Wherefore, holy brethren, partakers of the heavenly calling, consider the Apostle and High Priest of our profession, Christ Jesus. (Hebrews 3:1)

He lives! Hebrews continues, "Jesus Christ is always the same, yesterday, today, and yes, forever" (Hebrews 13:8). Christ Jesus is alive and He is the same today as He was yesterday, and as He will be forever. He is still healing countless numbers today through His Body, the Church.

The gospels show us that Jesus used many different healing streams as He healed individuals and multitudes. His ministry to the poor, outcast, demonized, or diseased was to preach and teach the Good News of the Kingdom, and heal them. In fact, Jesus told His disciples of that day to do the same (see Matthew 10:1, Luke 9:1, 6, Mark 6:7, 12-13, and 16:15-19). The Scriptures also show us that Jesus commanded His disciples to heal the sick, cast out demons, and raise the dead. The Great Commission indicates that the Lord's original disciples were to teach future disciples all that Jesus had first commanded them. Writes Matthew ". . . teaching them to observe all that I commanded you" (Matthew 28:20). His commands clearly included healing the sick.

If you have not been exposed to the scriptures on healing, begin today to gain knowledge of what you are entitled to through Christ. The promises are fulfilled in Christ. The Apostle Paul writes,

> For as many as may be the promises of God, in Him they are yes; wherefore also by Him is our Amen to the glory of God through us. (2 Corinthians 2:20)

Just as Moses laid his hands on Joshua and passed on the anointing, we can trace the anointing through the laying on of hands all the way back to the first apostles. Yes, the same anointing is passed down to ministers of the gospel today. When the Holy Spirit is present as ministers are ordained into the five-fold ministry, the ministry gifts are activated. Also, when believers are baptized in the fullness of the Holy Spirit, they are endued with power. Jesus tells His followers:

> But you will receive power when the Holy Spirit has come upon you, and you will be My witnesses in Jerusalem, in all Judea and Samaria, and to the ends of the earth. (Act 1:8)

Renew Your Mind

The Holy Spirit through John prays, "Beloved, I pray that in all respects you may prosper and be in good health, just as your soul prospers" (3 John 2). This verse points out that as our soul (our mind or thoughts, will and emotions) prospers, likewise our health and overall prosperity are to increase. Succinctly, as the mind is renewed, success in life and health follow—as you take in scriptures on healing, you develop understanding of the will of God and your faith begins to blossom.

Paul describes this foremost key to changing your life:

> And that you be renewed in the spirit of your mind, and put on the new self, which in {the likeness of} God has been created in righteousness and holiness of the truth. (Ephesians 4:23 24)

A renewed mind is the outcome of growing in the knowledge and understanding of God's Word and therefore, knowledge of Him. In like manner, a renewed mind will produce faith for the promises of God. "You are to not be conformed to the world, to its way of living, but be transformed by changing your way of thinking" (Romans 12:2 paraphrase). This begins by getting a new mindset toward the truth. If you do not guard your heart, and stay alert to what is happening in your mind—the attacks from without and within, you will experience mental and emotional issues—such as depression. Feed on the Word of God and be alert to what is transpiring in your mind. Do not give the devil an opportunity. Peter warns:

> Be sober and self-controlled. Be watchful. Your adversary the devil, walks around like a roaring lion, seeking whom he may devour. Resist him, firm in your faith . . . " (1 Peter 5:8-9)

One does not develop a renewed mind overnight, and faith for healing generally does not happen overnight either. We make a decision to pursue God through study of His Word, and opening ourselves for revelation from His Spirit. The term "renewing" is the Greek word *anakainosis*, and refers to a renovation, a redo, or complete change of mind. Mind is the word *nous* and carries the meaning of perceiving and understanding, even judging and comprehending. We see this used in Luke, "The He opened their minds (understanding), that they might understand the scriptures" (Luke 24:45 emphasis added).

The outcome of a renewed mind is a character change, holiness, and an increase in faith. Writes Paul, "So faith {comes} from hearing, and hearing by the word of Christ" (Romans 10:17). Notice faith comes from hearing and hearing. Faith grows in us through a process that comes from hearing the Word. The same process used in renewing your mind is at work to increase your faith. This happens from your meditation on the Word, as you read or hear it from ministers, tapes, books or your own mouth as you read the Bible. The number one way is reading and meditating from the Bible on your own. The process continues throughout your life as you grow in your walk with God.

Faith is the Key

Abraham appears in the faith hall of fame in Hebrews 11. Yet he did not automatically have strong faith. Paul tells us "Abraham "grew strong in faith." Paul explains,

> Yet, with respect to the promise of God, he did not waver in unbelief, but grew strong in faith, giving glory to God, and being fully assured that what He had promised, He was able also to perform. (Romans 4:20-21)

This same kind of faith is what is applied to receive healing by faith—faith that is unwavering, strong, fully assured of God's ability to provide what He promised, and faith that gives glory to God.

Whatever the individual's amount of faith, healing is available because God in His great omniscience made provision for us at the level at which we could obtain. Our job is to yield to His work in our lives and keep our eyes on the Healer, and not on the healing—or even the stream of healing that He uses.

The many and varied people of faith spoken of in the Word of God show us that we can obtain divine health from a number of approaches to God. One should not limit God to a certain stream of healing. He is greater than any method or knowledge; always, He meets us at our particular level. Many are looking to God for a miracle when they should be looking for steady increases in and a gradual return to health, "a state of recovery," such as is shown in scripture about the ten lepers in Luke 17 who, "as they were going they were cleansed;" and the healing of the Nobleman's son in John 4, of whom it is said, "he began to get better."

31

You will often see ministers tell the one being healed to do something he has not done before when the gifts of healings are in manifestation. Obedience results in healing miracles. It has been said, "Faith has feet." In other words, the healed one is to put his faith into action. Your beliefs are established as much by what you do as by what you know. Smith Wigglesworth, *The Apostle of Faith,*" was known to walk back and forth over and over quoting, "Faith is an act."

Jesus made clay and put it on the eyes of a blind man, telling him to go to the Pool of Siloam to wash. John records,

> When He had said this, He spat on the ground, and made clay of the spittle, and applied the clay to his eyes, and said to him, "Go, wash in the pool of Siloam" (which is translated, sent). And so he went away and washed, and came {back} seeing. (John 9:6 7)

Peter told the man at the Beautiful gate of the Temple to "rise up and walk" (Acts 3:6). The Prophet Elisha told his servant, Gehazi, to instruct Naaman, the leper, to wash seven times in the Jordan (2 Kings 5:10). In these instances, obedience resulted in healing miracles. I once asked a man to dance after I laid hands on him for healing of prostate cancer. I believe the Holy Spirit led me to ask the man to "do something that He had not done before to get something he had not had before." The man responded and reported later of his healing.

Often people will come for healing and then check their bodies instead of operating in faith. They must be taught to believe they have received regardless of what their senses tell them. Miracles happen and should be a part of the ministry of healing, but most people recover instead of receiving an instant manifestation. A young lady attended a session I taught on Christ the Healer. Although she was not sick, she wanted to learn about divine healing and build her faith. Shortly afterward, she was in an accident and was seriously injured. She lay on her back for several days confessing the Word of her healing. During a meeting with another minister, she was assisted to a healing line and took off her back brace when she received prayer, believing she was supernaturally healed of a crushed vertebra. She danced before the Lord in joy over her healing. Five months later, her intense pain returned. She came to my meeting in pain demonstrating the same symptoms. After I preached a message on our complete redemption and Christ's victory over the enemy, she came forward to have hands laid on her. She recognized that the enemy had tried to steal the Word (see Luke 8:12). Then she acted on her faith, bending over to touch her toes, and once more, her healing manifested. As far as I know, she has held on to it since then, quoting, "Distress will not rise up twice" (Nahum 1:9).

Jesus taught His disciples by example and Word and expected them to grow in faith. He expects the same from us. We are to grow in faith and in our ability to receive healing and anything else found in the promises of God. We might start out believing we have little faith, but we are to grow. Paul wrote to the Romans,

> For I say, through the grace given unto me, to every man that is among you, not to think [of himself] more highly than he ought to think; but to think soberly, according as God hath dealt to every man the measure of faith. (Romans 4:3)

Trust God that He has given you "the measure" of faith and will produce in you what He desires as you commit the measure of faith you have, and allow it to come forth. I used the example of Abraham's growth in faith because the scriptures indicate he grew in faith,

> Yet, with respect to the promise of God, he did not waver in unbelief, but grew strong in faith, giving glory to God (Romans 4:20)

.

Abraham came from a place of fear, a dependence on his own ability to preserve his life at the expense of his wife's chastity (Genesis 12 and 20), to a place of total dependence on God, even if it meant God had to raise someone from the dead to do it.

> By faith Abraham, when he was tried, offered up Isaac: and he that had received the promises offered up his only begotten [son], accounting that God [was] able to

raise [him] up, even from the dead; from whence also he received him in a figure. (Hebrews 11:17, 19)

We see this same progression of trust (faith) in God in the lives of the Patriarchs that followed Abraham. Isaac also lied about His wife, and Jacob stole his brother's birthright instead of trusting in God. However, as they walked with God, both grew in dependence on Him.

Most notably, Jacob, who would later be called Israel, wrestled with an angel of God until finally, the angel touched his thigh, and this place of strength became weak. Moses records, "And when he saw that he prevailed not against him, he touched the hollow of his thigh; and the hollow of Jacob's thigh was out of joint, as he wrestled with him" (Genesis 32:25). This forced Jacob to cling even more in faith for a blessing. He began to lean on, rely on, and trust in God. He knew that he could not face Esau, whom he had defrauded of his birthright, without first receiving God's blessing.

If you have revelation on God's love for you, then it is so much easier to receive healing.

Faith believes, speaks and acts like what God said is true. Our faith is so important to God, our trust in Him, that He will sometimes allow us to push the envelope, so to speak, until we are forced to have faith in Him. Wisdom writes, "Trust in the LORD with all your heart; and lean not unto your own understanding" (Proverbs 3:5). To trust God completely, is to know and have revelation on His great love for us, and His goodness toward us, and then to rest in it. If you have revelation on God's love for you, then it is so much easier to receive healing.

Faith believes, speaks and acts like what God said is true.

One of the main scriptures that prophesied the healing that God would make available to all who would believe and receive is found in Isaiah 53, the Great Redemptive Chapter. Writes Isaiah as He saw His glory, "Surely our sicknesses he hath borne, and our pains — he hath carried them" (Isaiah 53:4a). Your translation may say that he took our griefs and sorrows. The Hebrew words used in this scripture, *choli* and *macabe,* are most often translated in other scriptures as sickness and pains. In the New Testament, Matthew interprets Isaiah 53:4 for us, as he writes that Jesus fulfilled this passage by the prophet Isaiah—

34

quoting from Isaiah 53: "He took our infirmities and carried our diseases" (Matthew 8:17). I ask, is anyone left out of our? The Greek verb tense of Matthew 8:17 is that of continuing, not of a onetime event. And we know that "God is not a man that He should lie" (Numbers 23:19). As you see the many streams of healing that God has provided for us from which to receive, this alone should convince you of His desire for us to be whole.

Remember that healing has two parts: The God-ward side and the man-ward side. People need to first establish God's will in their hearts for healing, becoming firmly persuaded of God's will, not just His ability. Then they must learn how to receive from God—how to release their faith. Most of the time, absent a special manifestation of God's Spirit, people receive healing by faith. Again, faith comes by hearing, and if people do not take the time to build their faith, they will generally not be able to appropriate the grace of healing.

God does His part and we must do our part to appropriate all He has made available through the cross.

Two Sides of the Coin—The Godward and Manward Side of Wholeness

Jesus used a denarius with the image of Caesar, the Roman Emperor, to make a point. In answer to whether it was right to pay taxes or not, Jesus essentially said to give to Caesar what is his, and to God the things that are His (Luke 20:25). You might apply this to one side of the coin representing man, and the other side, God. Coins in the United States bear the image of a past President and the words, "In God We Trust." On the other side, the words "E Pluribus Unum" appear. The Latin term means "Out of the Many One."

Historically speaking, while designed to communicate the oneness of the original colonies, the term can certainly be applied doctrinally to oneness with God. The two aspects are the "manward side" of the coin, which is the authority of man who trusts in God, and the "Godward side," God making the many of mankind one in Him.

In the same manner, eternal life, salvation, in fact, all the benefits of our relationship and peace with God that we experience through Christ has two aspects, the Godward side, and the manward side. The Passover, God's work in the Atonement, and all the offerings and sacrifices all point to the work of Christ. God had a part in the shadow Christology, and man had a part. Man brought the sacrifices and complied with the obligations, and God accepted them as IOUs for the payment that He Himself would pay through Christ.

Now, we apply this Godward and manward side to all the benefits of the cross—health and prosperity as well as reconciliation—meaning all of the work of Christ. Sin was imputed to Christ on the cross—He was made sin. Sickness is a result of original and continued sin, and linked to sin and death because all sinned (Romans 5:12). Christ dealt with sickness at its root, which is sin. The manward side of healing receives by faith what was completed on the Godward side.

Too many are living by other peoples' experiences and their own feelings and failures instead of the Word. They limit the Word of God by allowing their experiences or circumstances to determine truth instead of embracing and standing firmly on the Word. They may see a doctor for healing while at the same time say that it must not be God's will to heal. Well, if it is God's will that they remain sick, why are they going to a doctor and getting out of His will? People do not always think, but instead rely on what they have been told by a person or even a minister who has not taken God at His Word. If sickness is truly God's will for us, then I expect sickness will exist in heaven because certainly His will is being done in heaven. We know that the Word of God says that there is no suffering in heaven.

> *If we want to see the supernatural, we must believe in the supernatural—we must believe God's Word, regardless of symptoms or circumstances.*

If we want to see the supernatural, we must believe in the supernatural—we must believe God's Word, regardless of symptoms or circumstances. He will honor our faith. Once you have established God's will in your life for divine health, it is time to learn how to release your faith. This includes learning how to receive healing—how to release your faith. First faith must be produced, and then released. You will find that you are either seeking to grow in faith and establish it, or releasing it. The cleansing and healing streams chapters that follow will help you with both.

CHAPTER THREE

Cleansing and Healing Stream 1

NEVER GIVE UP AND NEVER LOSE HEART—PRAY

For our own healing, of all the Cleansing and Healing Streams put forth, never forget that prayer is a believer's primary channel to receive from God. I have gone to Him in prayer and worship, and later realized that every pain had disintegrated. I believe in "soaking" in His Presence at every opportunity. We need to stay God-conscience at all times, keeping Him in the center of our thoughts; but as with any relationship, one-on-one quality time is when a relationship flourishes.

He will whisper the answer to you about what you seek, and if you do not hear the whisper, He may speak authoritatively—then a dream or vision, and yes, even a prophet may communicate your answer. Prayer is communion with the Living God. It is love at its best. Some call it loving on God. I have never loved on Him—kissed His face in worship—that I did not sense His great love as the force that compels my love. Love gives.

Before Christ took on flesh, the Jews prayed for one another to be healed. This is one reason some recognized Jesus as the Messiah, He healed people without prayer—not that He didn't pray in solitude, but He demonstrated authority over sickness—on a level with God. He never hesitated to speak and act like God would speak or act. This same distinction is for us today. God is with us. While we may act on behalf of others to take authority over sickness and command healing as Christ's representatives on Earth, we also can receive for ourselves in solitude through prayer. I also believe that when we pray for others, God hears. Some have experienced great power with God in prayer. The key is in expecting and persevering.

Jesus made a point about prayer and vindication from God. Tongue in cheek, He tells the story of a wicked judge, and then pronounces the difference in God! Notice that God will bring justice to those who cry to Him day and night:

Now He was telling them a parable to show that at all times they ought to pray and not to lose heart, saying, "In a certain city there was a judge who did not fear God and did not respect man."There was a widow in that city, and she kept coming to him, saying, 'Give me legal protection from my opponent.' "For a while he was unwilling; but afterward he said to himself, 'Even though I do not fear God nor respect man, yet because this widow bothers me, I will give her legal protection, otherwise by continually coming she will wear me out.'" And the Lord said, "Hear what the unrighteous judge said; now, will not God bring about justice for His elect who cry to Him day and night, and will He delay long over them? I tell you that He will bring about justice for them quickly. However, when the Son of Man comes, will He find faith on the earth?" (Luke 18:1-8)

Would you rather be found in faith orlacking faith when He comes? Waiting and watching, looking, asking seeking, knocking—that is a believer's way of life. Jesus explained,

Here's what I'm saying: Ask and you'll get; Seek and you'll find; Knock and the door will open. (Luke 11:9 MSG)

Winston Churchill gave a speech during World War II that is often quoted. In the sense of a biblical three-time emphasis, he spoke about withstanding the enemies of England:

Never give in—never, never, never, never, in nothing great or small, large or petty, never give in except to convictions of honour and good sense. Never yield to force; never yield to the apparently overwhelming might of the enemy. (Sir Winston Churchill, Speech, 1941, Harrow School)

Just as England had enemies threatening their very society and citizens' lives, believers have enemies that need withstanding. Be it sickness, oppression, poverty, persecution—whatever, we should never give up. Sir Edmund Hilary went up on stage after an unsuccessful attempt to climb Mt. Everest and declared to its picture: "Mt Everest, this time, you may have defeated me, but I will be back, for you remain the same size, and yet I will have grown bigger!" I say, "The bigger the battle, the bigger the victory." Never lose heart and faith—"This is the victory that overcomes the word, our faith" (1 John 5:4).

The Lord said to me very authoritatively on one occasion, "Will you trust Me?" I believe He asks this of all. In every situation that requires a stand, or exercise of more faith, I think of His Words. *Yes, Lord, I will trust You.*

They didn't thirst when he led them through the deserts; he
caused the waters to flow out of the rock for them; he split the
rock also, and the waters gushed out. (Isaiah 48:21)

CHAPTER FOUR

Healing Streams 2 & 3

THE HOLY SPIRIT AND POWER [2]

Distinctions exist in God's power and gifts. The gospels indicate that Jesus began His miracle ministry after John baptized Him in the Jordan River and the Holy Spirit came upon Him. He did not perform miracles because of His authority and power as the Son of God, but through the anointing of Holy Spirit at His baptism. Jesus was one hundred percent God and one hundred percent man, not fifty percent of each. Yet He came as a prophet of God, and operated on this earth as a man anointed by God with the Holy Spirit and power. Jesus proclaimed in the Synagogue,

> The Spirit of the Lord is upon Me, because He anointed me to preach the gospel to the poor. He has sent me to proclaim release to the captives, and recovery of sight to the blind, to set free those who are downtrodden, to proclaim the favorable year of the Lord. (Luke 4:18-19)

This verse tells us that God anointed Jesus with the Holy Spirit and with tangible power. Peter proclaimed something similar,

> You know of Jesus of Nazareth, how God anointed Him with the Holy Spirit and with power, and {how} He went about doing good, and healing all who were oppressed by the devil; for God was with Him. (Acts 10:38)

Many people are confused about healing because they believe it is only accomplished through the sovereignty of God, which would

---

[2] *E. W. Kenyon calls this Healing Methods One and Four in* Jesus the Healer, 36.

41

mean God's will on healing can vary. To be sovereign means to be supreme in power, and possess supreme dominion. God is sovereign ruler of the universe. But being healed sovereignly is more like getting a free sample or advertisement of His healing power that points us to God's sovereign will for all to be healed. If God's will were not constant, He would not be God. Samuel exclaims, "Also the Glory of Israel will not lie or change His mind; for He is not a man that He should change His mind" (1 Samuel 15:29). He does not change.

With the grace of God made available through the Atonement, all can receive healing by faith. However, as to healing through the sovereignty of God, God heals because He is God and wants to heal. Under the anointing, many may be healed in a meeting, and yet many others may go away without healing. The anointing of the Holy Spirit on a person may be a powerful anointing, and yet, some who are in desperate need of healing may not receive what they desire. *Remember, God is most often moved by faith and not by a person's desire.* Remember, God is most often moved by faith and not by a person's desire. It is true that under the anointing of the Holy Spirit, God will frequently heal according to His sovereignty—as the Spirit wills, but His anointing also does its work in all who believe. Isaiah proclaimed,

> So it will be in that day, that his burden will be removed from your shoulders and his yoke from your neck, and the yoke will be broken because of fatness. (Isaiah 10:27)

The fatness represents the anointing. Sickness is a yoke and can be a heavy burden, but the anointing of God demolishes the yoke.

When one sees friends or relatives with a disease that is not healed, or sees a few healed in a service, they think God only heals sovereignly, meaning whomever He chooses. No. He does, in His sovereignty, heal, but His will is for all to be healed, which is one explanation of why there are so many streams of healing available. Just as it is His will for all people to be saved, which includes the meaning of wholeness in this life, it is God's will to heal all people all the time. Similarly, all people do not act on God's Word and receive

His righteousness, and all do not receive healing. It does not negate His will when all do not believe, and when all are not healed.

God may single out a ministry or a person, and this person will have healings manifested. You may have heard where some have gone to a healing service or a revival and were healed. This is often a case of God intervening to advertise that He is God. The persons may or may not be Christians, and may not even have any faith evidenced. God heals many times to demonstrate His omnipotent power and His great mercy. You will often see people receiving Jesus as Lord as a result of this type of advertising as they witness a miracle of healing. Healing is like a loud call to dinner that draws people to the kingdom of God—what some call the dinner bell. Such special manifestations of power draw attention to God's omnipotence, and people decide that He is real. Even the hardened become believers when God's power to heal is evidenced. Many forget that Jesus went about teaching, preaching and healing according to Matthew 4:23 and 9:35. He healed everywhere He went. Many heard He was a healer and came for that reason alone, not because He was the Messiah.

The gifts of the Spirit show us that God has also provided another stream of healing for believers through the Holy Spirit:

> For to one is given the word of wisdom through the Spirit, and to another the word of knowledge according to the same Spirit; to another **faith** by the same Spirit, and to another **gifts of healing** by the one Spirit, and to another the **effecting of miracles**, and to another prophecy, and to another the distinguishing of spirits, to another {various} kinds of tongues, and to another the interpretation of tongues. But one and the same Spirit works all these things, distributing to each one individually just as He wills. (1 Corinthians 12:8-11 Emphasis added)

Notice from this passage that there are gifts of healing. Healing is actually plural in the Greek and should read gifts of "healings". Gain confidence. The Holy Spirit manifests as many gifts of the Spirit as there are diseases to heal. The Holy Spirit is pointing out throughout this chapter that the Body of Christ has been given gifts of the Spirit that are distributed in the body as the Spirit wills. They are sacred endowments.

Thank the Lord that He places you as He desires in the body, "All do not have gifts of healings, do they?" (1 Corinthians 12:30a). God does not want us to focus on only one mode of healing. He has placed many gifts in the body, but other ways to be healed exist.

Believers do not decide when the gifts of the Holy Spirit will be manifested. This is as the Spirit wills. We are merely vessels for Him to flow through. You may see that Jesus operated in the gifts. In fact, John's gospel says He had the "fullness of the Spirit without measure" (John 4:34). Yet, Jesus did not always operate in the gifts. He told Nathanael that before Phillip called Him, He saw him under the fig tree; and He told the woman at the well about her life in John 4, showing that He was operating in the word of knowledge described in 1 Corinthians 12. However, when Jesus cast the demon from the boy whose father came to Him, He asked the boy's father, "How long has this been happening to him?" (Mark 9:21). This shows us that at that moment, Jesus was not operating in the word of knowledge, as in the earlier examples.

They were so intent on being healed that they failed to realize they already were healed.

As I see the word of knowledge and word of wisdom in operation in the ministry entrusted to me, I frequently will be given a word of knowledge or wisdom. It is as the Spirit manifests His presence in this manner. It is evident to me that the gifts of the Spirit flow more freely in an atmosphere of love and compassion. Also in an atmosphere of faith and expectancy, the Spirit seems to more freely manifest Himself through these gifts. When the people are expecting, their level of faith is high, and the Lord is pleased. The writer of Hebrews extols, "Without faith, it is impossible to please God, for He who comes to God must believe that He is and that He is a rewarder of those who seek Him" (Hebrews 11:6).

The gifts of the Spirit are different from the power seen in the anointing on certain people, such as we read about in the ministries beginning with Jesus, and then on Paul and Peter, and whomever God chooses in His sovereignty. This type of anointing is seen in manifestation when people reach out by faith to receive such as is written about Jesus, who was anointed with the Holy Spirit and with power (Acts 10:38). The Holy Spirit anoints with power. The anointing on Peter was so strong that the people laid sick ones where Peter's shadow would fall on them. Luke records,

> And at the hands of the apostles many signs and wonders were taking place among the people; and they were all with one accord in Solomon's portico . . . to such an extent that they even carried the sick out into the streets, and laid them on cots and pallets, so that when Peter came by, at least his shadow might fall on any one of them. (Acts 5:12, 5:15)

I have personally had people come forward for ministry and knew by the Spirit that they had already been healed as they heard the message. They were so intent on being healed that they failed to realize they already were healed. Once I asked if their pain was gone, a smile always followed. Some receive healing from the anointing present as they sit in their chairs, some by hearing a different message that quickens their spirit, some by laying on of hands, some by having the sickness or demonic spirit (such as a spirit of fear) cast out, some by the prayer of agreement, and some by handkerchiefs that were in contact with the anointing as I preached and were taken to a sick or disturbed person. Faith is always an ingredient in these examples.

The anointing is the tangible substance of the Holy Spirit and can permeate anything and remain.

The anointing was so strong on Paul, miracles manifested from cloths saturated with the anointing and taken to a sick or demon-possessed person. Luke relates,

> And God was performing extraordinary miracles by the hands of Paul, so that handkerchiefs or aprons were even carried from his body to the sick, and the diseases left them and the evil spirits went out. (Acts 19:11-12)

The anointing is the tangible substance of the Holy Spirit and can permeate anything and remain. The substance of the anointing might be understood much as when one puts his head on a pillow where a spouse has slept, and the spouse's perfume has remained in the fabric. John G. Lake, a well known healing pioneer, tells of people experiencing the anointing when they received his newsletter. A woman with an issue of blood touched Jesus' hem and received this tangible substance, and her healing manifested. The anointing was so powerful that it saturated His clothing, even the fringe of His garment—the *tzitzit* of His *tallit* (prayer shawl). The Jews called the four corners of a *tallit, a* prayer shawl, wings. The Jews believed the Messiah would come with "healing in his wings" (Malachi 4:2). The cords and knots of the fringe *(tzitzit)* on the shawl indicated the commandments and God's name in obedience to (Numbers 15:38-39). The woman with the issue of blood pressed in and took hold of Jesus' *tzitzit*, His hem.

> And immediately Jesus, perceiving in Himself that the power {proceeding} from Him had gone forth, turned around in the crowd and said, "Who touched My garments?" (Mark 5:30). And they {began} to entreat Him that they might just touch the fringe of His cloak; and as many as touched {it} were cured. (Matthew 14:36)

When the anointing is present on a believer and comes into contact with any ungodliness, the ungodliness will have to yield. Sickness is an oppression of the enemy, and as such, is ungodly. It needs to be treated like ungodliness. Sickness has to go. It cannot stand against the anointing. Just as we saw in the cloths from Paul's body, even evil spirits had to go when they came into contact with the anointing.

But what is a believer to do if the gifts of the Spirit or a special manifestation of the Spirit are not in operation? Stand on the Word of God. When I first began to pray in faith for the sick in Healing School and speak the name of Jesus, I had very little understanding of the anointing, the gifts of the Spirit, or even the power in the name of Jesus. I merely did as the Word says. I laid hands on the sick and expected them to recover. God ministered to the people through me even in my infancy of faith. He often surprises me. When I have felt His power and anointing available, the people did not always receive it. And when I did not feel His power and anointing as being present—miracles have taken place. You will recall the story of how the power of God was present for healing but those present were not being healed because of unbelief:

> And it came to pass on a certain day, as he was teaching, that there were Pharisees and doctors of the law sitting by, which were come out of every town of Galilee, and Judea, and Jerusalem: and the power of the Lord was [present] to heal them. (Luke 5:17)

However, when persistent men of faith helped a friend to Jesus by taking off part of the roof and lowering the man down to Jesus, he was able to benefit from the power available. Faith activates the anointing.

People frequently brought me handkerchiefs to wear or to pray over as I ministered that could be taken to the sick. In one such instance, a lady took the handkerchiefs to a missionary in Africa. The lady wrote back of the healing and lifting of oppression that came from their use of the handkerchiefs. A lady who has recovered from cancer frequently brought in several handkerchiefs at a time to take to friends and relatives. The anointing truly removes burdens and destroys yokes.

The anointing is so tangible that it seems to permeate the prayer room where we intercessors gather. Sometimes it gets so thick during prayer that we feel a heavy weight. In my personal secret place, it is as though the very walls are saturated with God's Presence. As I trod my well-worn path to the secret place, I seem to sink deeper into the anointing. *Lord, we are coming to join You.*

They didn't thirst when he led them through the deserts; he caused the waters to flow out of the rock for them; he split the rock also, and the waters gushed out. (Isaiah 48:21)

CHAPTER FIVE

Healing Streams 4 & 5

THE PRAYER OF FAITH & ANOINTING WITH OIL[3]

The Prayer of Faith is often the mode used by the church for its members. It is typically called the prayer of faith because it indicates that this prayer is prayed for another in faith. James gives the formula:

> Is anyone among you sick? Let him call for the elders of the church, and let them pray over him, anointing him with oil in the name of the Lord and the prayer offered in faith will restore the one who is sick, and the Lord will raise him up, and if he has committed sins, they will be forgiven him (James 5:14-15)

The Greek word for sick is "*asthenei.*" It carries the meaning of a feeble one who is too sick or weak to help himself. This person is weak, perhaps exhausted and without strength, and therefore needs the prayers and the faith of others because he does not have enough of his own and is unable to go out to seek it. God had planned for the elders to help this weak one. Perhaps the weak one is not operating in the faith he has because pain has incapacitated him, he is feeble, depressed or feels guilt and condemnation. James says, "If he has committed sins, they will be forgiven him" (James 5:15). Sin and the associated guilt bring on sickness, and condemnation keeps the sick one bound

The enemy's hiss of sickness begins to sound louder than the Spirit of God to such a sick one.

by the enemy. It does not mean that sickness is always a result of sin—however, it could be the reason. But the source of sickness, its root, is sin. The enemy's hiss of sickness begins to sound louder than the Spirit of God to such a sick one.

We know that believers are to ask God for forgiveness, and He is faithful to forgive (1 John 1:9). In this instance, the prayer of faith

---

[3] *E. W. Kenyon calls this Healing Method Three in* Jesus the Healer, 37.

will help the person be healed on the faith of the ones praying. It will bring forgiveness as well, if the sick one confesses sin. I see many healed as a result of confessing sin, both overt sins of the flesh and hidden ones of the heart, such as unforgiveness. Note that the prayer of faith assumes that the elders who offer prayers for the sick one are in right standing with God, and they have faith to pray for healing for the one who is sick.

Anointing the sick one with oil is symbolic of anointing with the Holy Spirit. The oil also represents a consecration of the person to receive health for God's glory. The oil serves as a point of contact for the person to release his faith for healing. The oil itself does not have power. Again, the power is in the prayer of faith. James also tells us, "the earnest (heartfelt, continued) prayer of a righteous man makes tremendous power available (dynamic in its working)" (James 5:16 AMP).

In the New Testament, the disciples anointed with oil at the Lord's command. Mark records, "And they went out and preached that {men} should repent. And they were casting out many demons and were anointing with oil many sick people and healing them" (Mark 6:12 13). As the person is anointed with oil, faith is released as they envision the oil representing the anointing of the Holy Spirit.

In the Old Testament, the High Priest Aaron and his sons were anointed with special oil. God did not allow duplication of the oil for any other use. It symbolized the consecration of the priests to the Lord and the Lord's anointing upon them. The prophets also anointed kings whom God chose. The oil symbolizing the anointing of the Holy Spirit also represents our anointing as priests and kings. Peter reminds us,

> But you are a chosen race, a royal priesthood, a holy nation, a people for {God's} own possession, that you may proclaim the excellencies of Him who has called you out of darkness into His marvelous light. (1 Peter 2:9)

We are sons and daughters of God. In fact, as God's children we are "heirs of God, joint-heirs with Christ" (see Romans 8:17). The kingdom we have inherited is both to be enjoyed in this life and in the life to come. Sickness and sin is from the devil and has no place in our kingdom (none is in heaven). We are to reign in life through Christ (see Romans 5:21).

The devil usurped Adam's authority in the Garden of Eden. He did not come legally. Jesus exclaimed,

> Truly, truly, I say to you, he who does not enter by the door into the fold of the sheep, but climbs up some other way, he is a thief and a robber. The thief comes to steal, and kill, and destroy. I came that they might have life and might have it abundantly. (John 10:1, 10)

Abundant life is for this life, now! To give us this life, Jesus came legally in a body of flesh and blood, which God prepared for Him. The writer of Hebrews explains,

> Since then the children share in flesh and blood, He Himself likewise also partook of the same, that through death He might render powerless him who had the power of death, that is, the devil; and might deliver those who through fear of death were subject to slavery all their lives. (Hebrews 2:14-15)

Jesus has rendered the devil powerless by eliminating any fear of death, which is the root of all fear. The enemy has been disarmed (see Colossians 2:15). Jesus is triumphant and we are in Him. Therefore, we are triumphant since He has regained mankind's lost authority.

When the Western frontier was in its infancy, ranchers sometimes used land that had not been developed to graze their herds of cattle. Subsequently, settlers came into the territory and began to farm the undeveloped land that had been used for the ranchers as grass for their herds. The settlers put up fences on their property to keep in their domestic livestock and keep out unwanted predators. The settlers claimed rightful ownership to the land based on the fact they farmed and lived on the land. The settlers were called squatters, and their right to the land was called squatter's rights. The devil has only a squatter's rights in this kingdom. He did not legally inherit any authority, and Jesus has given us His authority to deal with the usurper and deceiver until Jesus permanently deals with him, throwing him into the lake of fire. We need to kick the devil off our property and take down the fences (the bondage of sickness). We have authority in the name of Jesus to do this. We are seated with Him in heavenly places in Christ (see Ephesians 2:6).

According to James 5:1, as we anoint a sick person with oil, we are in essence, consecrating them and praying the prayer of faith for their recovery. This is taking back possession of their bodies for the Lord.

The Holy Spirit gives life to our body, and the oil symbolizes His power at work in us. Paul encourages,

> But if the Spirit of Him who raised Jesus from the dead dwells in you, He who raised Christ Jesus from the dead will also give life to your mortal bodies through His Spirit who indwells you. (Romans 8:11)

Mortal does not mean a dead body, but a body that is subject to death because our current bodies are not immortal. When the sick one is anointed, it symbolizes the Holy Spirit's power at work to quicken his body to health. The prayer of faith will restore the one sick. The oil will remind the sick one that he is anointed, that he is a child of God and as such, a queen or king, consecrated for God's purpose.

As a part of my ministry to the sick, I keep oil available to anoint them. And even if I must travel to where they are, I take oil with me to anoint them. I believe strongly in establishing a point of contact for the sick to use for exercising their faith, and activating the anointing. The entire process outlined in James 5 may not be in operation; for example, the person may not need to confess sins. But when the person is anointed with oil in the name of Jesus, and prayer is made to God in Jesus' name, or the name of Jesus is used in taking authority over the sickness, healing will manifest. The name of Jesus represents His Person. It is not used as a magic formula and may not even have to be spoken aloud at times. But since I am fully confident that I am in His Person and He is in me, then I may pray or speak to a situation without consciously realizing I have not spoken His name, only acted in it! As His representative, an ambassador, I have boldness to act for Him.

CHAPTER SIX

Healing Stream 6

THE LAYING ON OF HANDS[4]

Laying on of hands is a fundamental doctrine of the church as listed in Hebrews 6:2. As such, it should not be ridiculed as some have, but held in esteem. Biblical examples exist of laying on of hands for reasons other than healing, such as ordainment. However, all indicate the power of God is transferred in the laying on of hands. As hands are laid on the person, they serve as a point of contact for releasing faith and transmission of the power of God. Through the laying on of hands, God transmits the healing anointing by the power of divine grace operating in and through the person. Since Jesus did not lay hands on everyone, neither should we. We are to be led by the Holy Spirit in receiving and in ministering to others.

God gave the Holy Spirit through the laying on of hands by believers. Dr. Luke writes, "And when Paul had laid his hands upon them, the Holy Spirit came on them, and they {began} speaking with tongues and prophesying" (Acts 19:6). This practice is still effective today as believers receive the baptism in the Holy Spirit through the laying on of hands. People testify of also receiving the baptism in the Holy Spirit in the privacy of their homes and in church services. Exceptions such as these are shown in the Bible in Acts 2 and 10. Therefore, we know that exceptions exist to receiving the baptism of the Holy Spirit other than through the laying on of hands. However, we could agree that laying on of hands is one fundamental method for receiving baptism in the Holy Spirit.

Paul reminded Timothy of the gift received when Paul laid his hands on him, "And for this reason I remind you to kindle afresh the gift of God which is in you through the laying on of my hands" (2 Timothy 1:6). In the book of Acts, God consecrated Barnabus and

---

[4] *E. W. Kenyon calls this Healing Method Two in* Jesus the Healer, 36, 37.

Saul (Paul) for work, which the Holy Spirit called them to do. Luke recounts,

> And while they were ministering to the Lord and fasting, the Holy Spirit said, "Set apart for Me Barnabas and Saul for the work to which I have called them." Then, when they had fasted and prayed and laid their hands on them, they sent them away. (Acts 13:2 3)

These men were being set apart for the ministry by the laying on of hands. In the Old Testament, Moses laid his hands on Joshua, and The Holy Spirit filled Joshua with the Spirit of Wisdom, Moses writes, "Now Joshua the son of Nun was filled with the spirit of wisdom, for Moses had laid his hands on him" (Deuteronomy 34:9). We see in this scripture that one man's anointing was imparted (released) to another through the laying on of hands.

Paul cautioned Timothy not to lay hands on someone too hastily (1 Timothy 5:22). This is also true in ministry to others. If the person's faith is not quickened, or they have not been taught the truth of the Good News, then when we lay hands on them for healing, they cannot appropriate the power of God available. Their faith may suffer as a result. Many ministers will not lay hands on someone until they have sat under their teaching and are ready to release their faith when hands are laid on them.

In contrast to asking for prayer for the recovery of a sick person, a synagogue official name Jairus asked Jesus to come and lay His hands on Jairus' daughter. Jairus recognized that the healing anointing was transmitted through the laying on of Jesus' hands;

> And one of the synagogue officials named Jairus came up, and upon seeing Him, fell at His feet, and entreated Him earnestly, saying, "My little daughter is at the point of death; {please} come and lay Your hands on her, that she may get well and live." (Mark 5:23)

Jairus understood that the healing power of God flowed through the laying on of hands. Another instance of Jesus laying His hands on a person for healing is the case of the leper to whom Jesus said, *"I am willing"* (Mathew 8:2). Matthew shows Jesus healing frequently and in large numbers. He writes, "And when the sun was setting, all who had any sick with various diseases brought them to Him; and laying His hands on everyone of them, He was healing them" (Luke 4:40).

These few instances I have included show us that Jesus laid his hands on sick people and healed them. Jesus also used other methods for healing the sick. He sometimes spoke to the sickness. He always spoke to demons to cast them out, as did the disciples He commissioned. But also the anointing causes demons to flee (see Acts 19:12). Our authority as believers enables us to rebuke and cast out demons. This is granted to every believer (see also Cleansing and Healing Stream 9, Deliverance and Healing).

Part of Jesus' commission to believers is to go into the entire world, preach the gospel and lay hands on the sick. Mark gives His command,

> And these signs will accompany those who have believed: in My name they will cast out demons, they will speak with new tongues; they will pick up serpents, and if they drink any deadly {poison,} it shall not hurt them; they will lay hands on the sick, and they will recover. (Mark 16:17 18)

This verse indicates getting people healed is to be a part of their believing. Notice the verse said "those who have believed." While believers in this age do go into the world to preach the gospel, they often leave the healing part of the great commission out. Based on the full context of the great commission, all believers can expect to lay hands on the sick and see them healed. Healing is definitely to be a part of the believer's ministry.

Our authority as believers enables us to rebuke and cast out demons.

The anointing on a person affects the degree of power administered by the laying on of hands, but all believers can merely do the Word and see people recover. Believers have an anointing on the inside. The same Holy Spirit in the life of Jesus lives in us. John explains, "But you have an anointing from the Holy One, and you all know" (have received real knowledge, my emphasis) (1 John 2:20, 27). Paul reminds us that Christ is in us (Colossians 1:27).

I previously mentioned that God supernaturally anoints some ministers with a tangible anointing for healing. I am aware of this many times when I lay hands on people. As the power of God streams in and through me, I may become light-headed, and if I lay hands on a number of people in succession, I require assistance to stand. Of notable mention though, I have sometimes felt nothing and yet God performed a miracle. One man could not eat very much as a result of having had ninety percent of his stomach removed. He said that he was growing weaker and weaker from lack of food. I spent little time praying for him. I merely laid my hands on his stomach and thanked God for giving him a new stomach (be led by the Spirit about laying hands on the opposite sex). He reported the next day that he could eat a full plate of Mexican food. He steadily increased in strength after that.

In another instance, a person dear to me was taken to the emergency room with what he believed was a heart attack. I left him in charge of another, but not without first laying my hands on his heart area and thanking God for healing him. I again did not feel the power of God as I laid hands on him and prayed. However, he took a big breath and looked up at me in amazement. He later told me that all his pain left when I laid hands on him and prayed. The heart attack was documented, but he came home from the hospital a couple of days later.

I often set this person up for healing. I would ask him if he believed in prayer, and when he said yes, I would pray. In a separate instance, God healed one of his legs that had been paralyzed due to a stroke, when I prayed for him and spoke life to his leg. He lifted it high and shouted with amazement. He could not keep from showing amazement. Keep in mind, I have fasted and prayed for God to increase the anointing and use me as an instrument of His mercy.

The prayer of faith administered with the laying on of hands is powerful. It helps the faith of some as they feel the tangible anointing of power going into them. Some fall or stagger under the power, and some merely will themselves to fall and soak in the anointing. It has been said that some people are trained to fall. Perhaps this is true, but whether the person falls because of the power of God or because they want to receive all they can as the anointing works in them, God will meet them at their level of faith, if faith is present. This level of healing requires the least amount of faith to receive as any other method.

In other instances where for example, someone has asked me to lay hands on them for minor complaints of headache or upset stomach, it amazes me how that person will receive quickly and be free from pain, and yet another right beside them who wants to get in on the healing power available, requires more ministry. I believe that the level of pain and personal anxiety, or fear is the culprit. In this instance, I speak the Word, allowing the Holy Spirit to lead me, sometimes rebuking the pain and using the Word of God to minister compassion first. Paul reminds us, "Faith works through love" (Galatians 5:6). If a person is in fear, their faith will not work. Fear is having more faith in the enemy than God. You may have heard the acronym, False Evidence Appearing Real. I once had a lady come for healing who had seen cancer in her immediate and extended family. She had been diagnosed with a lump in her breast. Fear was so evident that it could be observed. I required her to sit under my teaching, and then rebuked the spirit of fear. She said that the fear left. She reported back that the cancer was gone as well.

I was once very surprised by how the Holy Spirit manifested Himself as I laid hands on a lady for a heart condition. I merely touched her on her jaw with my fingertips, but something like electricity shot through my fingers. It so caught me off guard that I pulled away, but then put my fingers back on her face, and felt it again. She was also surprised, and reported later that she was healed— not only healed, but so full of energy that she cleaned her house for nearly twenty-four hours. She and her husband testified to her new-found energy. We just cannot limit the Holy Spirit. This was an unusual case, and I have not experienced that particular type of manifestation of the healing anointing again, but I have witnessed the anointing in different instances accomplish healing.

Recently a dear friend broke a bone and dislodged it such that it pressed against her clavicle. Her doctor took an x-ray, put her in a shoulder brace, and referred her to a specialist for surgery. She was having pain at night and difficulty sleeping. As she recounted this to me, my heart went out to her, and I said, "I just can't stand to think of you having to have surgery. May I pray for you?" She said, "Of course." As I laid hands on the spot where the bone was sticking out, and thanked God for healing her, she said, "I felt it move. I believe it is healed." She threw away the shoulder brace and began to confess her healing. This is an example of releasing one's faith for healing. Although her pain left immediately, later in the week, she recounted how it began to throb again. She spoke to it and thanked God for her healing. The pain left again. She went to the specialist later in the week, and he looked at the x-rays of the break. But when he examined her, he told her the bone was not broken, and asked why she was in his office! She told him about her healing and how she held on to it. He mentioned that faith could work sometimes. Some doctors are believers in the power of God, and some acquiesce only to the potential of prayer and faith. I was so pleased that not only did my friend not have to have surgery, but was able to give such a wonderful testimony of the Lord's goodness to her doctor.

During a church service, a minister anointed in this manner, may call sick people forward for healing, and the power of God is transmitted through the minister's hands as they make contact with the people. This is an excellent example of how God meets the people at their individual level of faith. When hands are laid on the sick person, the hands are a point of contact for releasing faith for healing.

God wants people to be healed. Whether they receive it by faith, the laying on of hands, the anointing or special gifts of the Spirit, prayer of agreement, anointing with oil, or any other method, all healing is from God and is appropriated by faith.

CHAPTER SEVEN

Healing Stream 7

THE PRAYER OF UNITY AND AGREEMENT [5]

Another stream of healing is available in the prayer of unity and agreement. In this example, the sick person is not so weak that he needs to call for the elders to pray over him. He is not confined to bed, but his faith appears greater when mixed with another's faith to activate the anointing. This person would take his faith and unite it with another's in agreement with the Word of God. The prayer of agreement is often cited from a verse in Matthew, which in reality, applies to correctly interpreting scripture! Jesus said,

> Again I say to you, that if two of you agree on earth about anything that they may ask, it shall be done for them by My Father who is in heaven. (Matthew 18:19)

Ask yourself, why would the prayer of three mean more to God than one person's prayer? True, a corporate anointing is powerful in prayer—as with the prayer of faith in James 5, but Jesus meant that an agreement of two or three is in the context of interpretation of the Word. Two or three witnesses established a fact in a Jewish court of law (Deuteronomy 19:15). When two or three agree in an interpretation, it is backed up

Keys represent authority and stewardship

by heaven, and also applies to using the Keys of the Kingdom. Keys represent authority and stewardship. Thus, what we have commonly used as a prayer of agreement is a reference to correctly interpreting the scriptures. This is further illustrated in "Prohibit and permit," which is the rabbinic meaning of bind and loose. Jesus said,

---

[5] *E. W. Kenyon calls this Healing Method Five in* <u>Jesus the Healer, 37, 38.</u>

I will give you the keys of the kingdom of heaven; and whatever you bind (declare to be improper and unlawful) on earth must be what is already bound in heaven; and whatever you loose (declare lawful) on earth must be what is already loosed in heaven. (Matthew 16:19 AMP, Matthew 18:18)

The Noahide laws (Acts 15:13-20) show us that the early church ruled not to require converts to Christ to be circumcised. They allowed (loosed) them to abide by the seven Noahide laws of Genesis 9; i.e. based on the Word of God, two or three leaders agreed on the entry of non-Jews into fellowship, and Heaven backed up the early church's ruling. **They did not make a ruling contrary to the revealed will of God.**

This explanation does not rule out using the keys of the kingdom powerfully in our everyday walk as we establish the revealed will of God on Earth and "in the heavenly places." When we speak by the Spirit, we establish on Earth the revealed will of God in heavenly places, where we are seated in union with Christ "over all rule and authority and power and dominion, and every name that is named, not only in this age but also in the one to come" (see Ephesians 1:19-21, 2:6). One of the church's assignments is to establish God's revealed will on earth and in the heavenly places through prayer and declaration. Paul explains:

So that the manifold wisdom of God might now be made known through the church to the rulers and the authorities in the heavenly places. (Ephesians 3:6)

As to the "principle of corporate anointing and agreement" with the Word, it still holds true. The agreement is for whatever is available to the believer from salvation such as healing, deliverance, safety, prosperity and preservation. "To agree" comes from the Greek word "*symphoneo*" and as it sounds, it is a word indicating harmony. It is two people saying the same thing in harmony, a symphony. Based on the law in Deuteronomy, two or three witnesses established a fact (Deuteronomy 17:6). Jesus points to this in Matthew,

But if he does not listen {to you,} take one or two more
with you, so that by the mouth of two or three witnesses
every fact may be confirmed. (Matthew 18:16)

The mouth is a singular word but the speakers are plural. This means
the speakers are in agreement. The two or three speak with one
mouth, saying the same thing. This can be a powerful prayer. In
marriage, a prayer in unity is especially powerful. Unity brings the
blessing. Moses writes:

Behold, how good and how pleasant it is for brothers to
dwell together in unity! It is like the precious oil upon
the head, coming down upon the beard, even Aaron's
beard, coming down upon the edge of his robes. It is
like the dew of Hermon coming down upon the
mountains of Zion; for there the LORD commanded the
blessing--life forever. (Psalm 133)

Unity keeps out strife, which is a hindrance to healing and answered
prayer. In marriage, the two are one flesh, and when united in the
Lord, they are in one Spirit. Paul writes to Corinth, "But the one who
joins himself to the Lord is one spirit with Him" (1 Corinthians 6:17).

The prayer of unity is a prayer of faith also. As juxtaposed
with the prayer of faith shown in James 5, the prayer of unity has great
power because the corporate anointing and faith of the two or three is
united to produce greater faith.

Jesus described the Word as a seed (Luke 8:11). He said even
small faith can move a mountain, and compared the faith necessary to
do a great work to the size of a mustard seed (Matthew 17:29). The
Word, which is the seed, is planted to produce by confessing it. When
two confess the Word in a prayer of unity, mixing it with faith, great
power is made available. Faith confessions plant the seed for whatever
is needed.

Often the prayer of unity is used for needs in other areas of
our lives. God did not make us to function independently from others
in the Body. That is why He gave individual gifts and types of

ministries. Paul explained that each joint in the Body of Christ has a supply:

> But speaking the truth in love, we are to grow up in all aspects of Him who is the head, even Christ from who the whole body being fitted and held together by that which every joint supplies, according to the proper working of each individual part, causes the growth of the body for the building up of itself in love. (Ephesians 4:15-16)

I have had instances where even though I know and operate in the authority of the Lord Jesus, I had to get another person to help me deal with something. The only answer I have for this is just as stated above. We are to help one another, and bear one another's burdens, and thus fulfill the Law of Christ (see Galatians 6:10). One way of thinking of this is that the anointing and gifts of the Spirit in which we are entrusted are for others. We must use our faith for ourselves and seek help from others in the body as the Lord leads.

We are to help one another, and bear one another's burdens, and thus fulfill the Law of Christ

CHAPTER EIGHT

Healing Stream 8

CELEBRATION OF COMMUNION

Jesus gave the Lord's Supper (as the Apostle Paul referred to Communion), to the church to bring us to remembrance of His death for us, and the Covenant He ratified through His blood on our behalf. He enacted the living parable of the gift of His body as the ultimate sacrifice during Passover in order to demonstrate that He was to become our Passover Lamb. During the Lord's Supper, we celebrate this New Covenant. In partaking of the bread and the wine, believers are mindful of the body and blood of Christ. Therefore, communion has two elements. People often see both elements as for the remission of sin, but just as the Hebrews smeared the Passover Lamb's

Redemption includes complete deliverance from lack, sickness, sin and fear of death.

blood on the doorpost for protection and deliverance, and ate its body for strength and healing, Communion brings to mind the Lamb's body and blood. Jesus did more than become sin on the cross for our justification— He also became sickness, and became poverty. He removed sin and sickness, defeated poverty and overcame death.

Throughout the Word, the forgiveness of sin and removal of sickness are linked together. Redemption includes complete deliverance from lack, sickness, sin and fear of death. One argument pertaining to redemption from sickness comes as a result of people not being healed at the same time as they believe. Paul explains the Word of faith,

> That if you confess with your mouth Jesus {as} Lord, and believe in your heart that God raised Him from the dead, you shall be saved. (Romans 10:9)

Then why is a believer still sick once saved? If sin is defeated through the work of the cross, then why not sickness? The answer is found in understanding the work of redemption. We have been taught that being "saved," the Greek word "*Sozo*", and "salvation." the Greek word "Soteria" mean saved, healed, safe, removed from danger, delivered, made whole, and prospered. What we have failed to see is that salvation, or being saved, is for this life, and not for heaven. Jesus said, "I came to give you life and life more abundantly" (John 10:10b). Securing our place in Heaven, looking forward to "the new heaven and new earth," has to do with knowing God, and believing we are made right with Him through the faith of Jesus Christ.

One can trace the origin of the different terms in the Old Testament and the New. The saints in the Old Testament looked forward to having their names written in the Book of Life, and so do we New Testament saints. We see concretely that being saved is being made whole, which is what the Savior demonstrated while on this earth, and continues to do through His Body today. He states his mission so clearly in Luke 4. The mission applies to now, not heaven or the age to come.

> The Spirit of the Lord is upon me, because he hath anointed me to preach the gospel to the poor; he hath sent me to heal the brokenhearted, to preach deliverance to the captives, and recovering of sight to the blind, to set at liberty them that are bruised, to preach the acceptable year of the Lord. (Luke 4:18:19 KJV)

Eternal life now and in the age to come is through knowing God and His Son Jesus Christ—believing in Him. Being saved—made whole—is obtained by knowing His Word, receiving its benefits, and doing the Word in this life.

The righteousness imparted to the believer is an inward experience of being reborn and brought into sonship, and a continual working out of what was received, which is the process of sanctification. As one's mind is renewed on the righteousness imparted by Christ, the believer is able to appropriate fully all of the blessings provided by God through Christ in the Eternal Covenant.

From Scripture, we see that hunger and thirst for righteousness will be satisfied. Jesus said, "Blessed are those who hunger and thirst for righteousness, for they shall be satisfied" (Matthew 5:6). Jesus said, *"They shall be satisfied."* I believe Jesus is talking about those who truly hunger and thirst for righteousness, which is only satisfied by believing in Him and abiding in Him. In doing so, the believer enters the Covenant and literally becomes a part of His body, partaking of His body and His blood. His blood ratified the covenant and His body made a way into the Holy of Holies, a new and living way through His flesh (see Hebrews 10:20).

To a Samaritan woman who Jesus met at Jacob's well, He said,

> Jesus said to her, If you knew the gift of God, and who it is that says to you, Give me to drink; you would have asked of him, and he would have given you living water. (John 4:10)

Jesus said to another group that He is living bread, "I am the bread of life. He who comes to me will never be hungry. And he who believes in Me will never thirst anymore" (John 6:35). He alone satisfies our hunger and thirst. He said, ". . . The bread that I give for the life of the world is my flesh" (John 6:36). In my book, Types and Shadows, I explained:

Eating and drinking identified with the body and the blood of Christ is portrayed in eating the bread and drinking the wine of communion. An example of the "bread and wine of righteousness" is found in the story of Abraham and Melchizedek. Follow this beautiful account:

> And when Abram heard that his relative had been taken captive, he led out his trained men, born in his house, three hundred and eighteen, and went in pursuit as far as Dan. And he divided his forces against them by night, he and his servants, and defeated them, and pursued them as far as Hobah, which is north of Damascus. And he brought back all the goods, and also brought back his relative Lot with his possessions, and also the women, and the people. Then after his return from the defeat of Chedorlaomer and the kings who were with him, the king of Sodom went out to meet him at the valley of Shaveh (that is, the King's Valley). And

Melchizedek king of Salem brought out bread and wine; now he was a priest of God Most High. And he blessed him and said, "Blessed be Abram of God Most High, Possessor of heaven and earth; And blessed be God Most High, who has delivered your enemies into your hand." And he gave him a tenth of all (Genesis 14:14-20).

The King of Salem means King of Peace. Peace is *shalom* in Hebrew. The root word for Salem is based on *shalom*. It means to be whole or set right—at peace (Strong 7965). That means nothing missing and nothing broken. This includes the meaning of wholeness. Jesus suffered the chastisement for our peace—our well being (Isaiah 53:5). In the Hebrew meaning of Shalom, peace with God implies also having peace with others. Wholeness includes (1) accepting oneself, (2) loving others, and (3) entering into a right relationship with God. A right relationship with God is precluded by a right relationship with others. On the Day of Atonement for example, the people believed that God forgave their sins against Him, but sins against others were satisfied when one's brother was satisfied that restitution had been made.

Melchizedek means king of the right, of the natural or moral and prosperity (Strong 4442). Being king of righteousness and peace, he is a portrait of Messiah, the Lord Jesus. "Abraham in turn gave him a tenth of the spoils. 'Melchizedek' means 'King of Righteousness.' 'Salem' means 'Peace.' So, he is also 'King of Peace'" (Hebrews 7:2 MSG).

Notice Melchizedek brought out bread and wine, prefiguring the Eucharist (Lord's Supper) with Christ our Passover:

Melchizedek makes a brief and mysterious appearance in the narrative as king of that Jerusalem where Yahweh will choose to dwell as priest of the Most High before the Levitical priesthood was established. In the bread and wine offered to Abraham it sees an image of the Eucharist and even a foreshadowing of the Eucharistic sacrifice (New Jerusalem Bible Genesis 14:18g).

Our righteousness comes from the blood of Jesus, the wine. Our healing comes from His broken body, the bread. The wine represents His blood for the inner man, our righteousness and uprightness before God. The bread represents His body, which is for the whole person, our soul and physical salvation. In other words, the blood of Jesus is for the sin nature of the spirit, and the body of Jesus is for the total mental and physical health. Remember, the Israelites ate the entire roasted Passover lamb for its healing and sustaining properties (Exodus 12:10).

The blood of Christ Jesus, as represented in the wine, signified removal of sin. His body, represented in the bread, signifies the healing and removal of sickness.

> Surely He has borne our griefs (sicknesses, weaknesses, and distresses) and carried our sorrows and pains [of punishment], yet we [ignorantly] considered Him stricken, smitten, and afflicted by God [as if with leprosy].But He was wounded for our transgressions, He was bruised for our guilt and iniquities; the chastisement [needful to obtain] peace and well-being for us was upon Him, and with the stripes [that wounded] Him we are healed and made whole. (Isaiah 53:4-5)

Healed is the Hebrew word *Rapha,* which means to be cured or made whole. Through His body we are healed and through His blood we are forgiven. We are reconciled and have peace with God through His sacrifice (Romans 5:1). In Exodus 15:26, God declares, "I Am Adonai Rapha, the Lord your Healer." I have substituted "Adonai" out of reverence for the Divine Name of God.

We receive the blessings through Christ, our High Priest on the order of Melchizedek. We are made right (upright) before God through the blood of Jesus. "Much more then, having now been justified by His blood, we shall be saved from the wrath of God through Him" (Romans 5:9). Peter calls the blood precious and explains,

> Knowing that you were not redeemed with perishable things like silver or gold from your futile way of life inherited from your forefathers, but with precious

blood, as of a lamb unblemished and spotless, {the blood} of Christ. (1 Peter 1:18-19).

Paul reinforces this truth as he warns of days ahead, and speaks of the blood as God's blood:

Be on guard for yourselves and for all the flock, among which the Holy Spirit has made you overseers, to shepherd the church of God which He purchased with His own blood. (Acts 20:28)

The blood, which the wine represents, and the Bread, which represents His body do not have intrinsic power. The power for healing in the communion is in remembering. The bread and wine are a point of contact for releasing faith. If you can learn to release your faith when you receive the communion elements, herein is the power. You call Jesus to remembrance and rejoice—your sin and your sickness have been carried away (Christian 84-86)

Our Father in Heaven is a God of total salvation. God does not want us redeemed and left sick or poor. David blessed the Lord in song for His goodness:

Bless the LORD, O my soul; and all that is within me, {bless} His holy name. Bless the LORD, O my soul, and forget none of His benefits; Who pardons all your iniquities; who heals all your diseases; Who redeems your life from the pit; who crowns you with lovingkindness and compassion; Who satisfies your years with good things, {so that} your youth is renewed like the eagle. (Psalms 103:1-5)

Sin and sickness are often shown as inseparable because sickness came when sin entered. Jesus ministered to a paralytic whose friends lowered him through a roof to get to Jesus: "And Jesus seeing their faith said to the paralytic, "My son, your sins are forgiven" (Mark 2:9). When criticized for His actions, Jesus said, "Which is easier, to say to the paralytic, 'Your sins are forgiven'; or to say, 'Arise, and take up your pallet and walk'?"(Mark 2:16-17). Later, as he dined, more criticism was leveled at Him:

> "Why is He eating and drinking with tax gatherers and sinners?" And hearing this, Jesus said to them, "{It is} not those who are healthy who need a physician, but those who are sick; I did not come to call the righteous, but sinners." (Mark 2:16-17)

Jesus is showing us that sin and sickness are of the same root. Healing is available for both, but we need to appropriate it. God taught the Israelites this principle. In the Exodus story, the elements of the Exodus Passover memorial were the flesh and the blood of the lamb. The lamb had to be examined and determined to be without blemish, then slain. Each family was to eat from the one lamb, and the blood applied to the doorposts and lintel so that the destroyer, the angel of death, would pass over the first born of the Israelites, striking only the Egyptians. The blood served as a covering so that the plague "passed over" the Israelites. God commanded the Passover to be remembered as a feast and memorial. The Israelites were to look back and remember the Lord delivered them and to be grateful for His salvation. The Israelites ate the lamb for strength and healing for their journey from Egyptian bondage, a type of sin and the world.

In the New Testament we have the communion as a feast and memorial. We are to look back on the cross at our redemption and remember the power of the body and the blood of Christ Jesus. Just as in the Exodus, when the Israelites ate the flesh of the lamb and smeared the blood on the doorposts and lintel, the body and blood of Jesus are our protection, redemption, deliverance, and healing today. The power for healing is not found in the actual elements of wine or the bread that represent the body and the blood of Christ. The power *God does not want us redeemed an left sick or poor* for healing is in identification with the sufferings of Christ for our deliverance and healing. We see that God has put away sin and sickness from us by putting them on Jesus. We see that God has provided for our complete redemption, and by faith, we receive it. In communion, we remind ourselves of the New Covenant made in His blood. We ask the Holy Spirit to empower our eating of the elements if we wish, and the bread and wine are a point of contact for releasing faith. This is a time to call Jesus to remembrance, and rejoice that God dealt with sins and sicknesses through Christ.

During His passion, the Romans beat Jesus' body and crucified Him so His blood flowed. In eating bread and drinking wine, we receive anew the power for healing by His body, and forgiveness by His blood, which was shed for our sins, and still may be received— salvation which includes healing. Writes Paul,

> For I received from the Lord that which I also delivered to you, that the Lord Jesus in the night in which He was betrayed took bread; and when He had given thanks, He broke it, and said, "This is My body, which is broken for you; do this in remembrance of Me." In the same way {He took} the cup also, after supper, saying, "This cup is the new covenant in My blood; do this, as often as you drink {it,} in remembrance of Me." For as often as you eat this bread and drink the cup, you proclaim the Lord's death until He comes. Therefore whoever eats the bread or drinks the cup of the Lord in an unworthy manner shall be guilty of the body and the blood of the Lord. But let a man examine himself, and so let him eat of the bread and drink of the cup. For he who eats and drinks, eats and drinks judgment to himself, if he does not judge the body rightly. For this reason many among you are weak and sick, and a number sleep. But if we judged ourselves rightly, we should not be judged. But when we are judged, we are disciplined by the Lord in order that we may not be condemned along with the world.
> (1 Corinthians 11:23 32)

Notice that Christians get weak, sick and sleep when they do not judge the body rightly. Those who sleep, sleep (die) because they do not walk in love, and do not judge the body rightly. If we will examine ourselves, we will not come into condemnation and become sick or die. About death, Jesus said,

> Truly, truly, I say to you, he who hears My word, and believes Him who sent Me, has eternal life, and does not come into judgment, but has passed out of death into life. (John 5:24)

Paul extols, "O DEATH, WHERE IS YOUR VICTORY? O DEATH, WHERE IS YOUR STING?" (1 Corinthians 15:55). The believer sleeps (because death for a believer is but a passage into life), but unbelievers die apart from God, being subject to the sting of death. The sting of death is gone for the believer, but why would anyone cut their life short? Let us honor Christ's body now.

Paul further tells the Corinthians to not eat and drink in an *unworthy manner*. Remember that by the stripes that Jesus took, we were healed. Believers are brethren, meaning of the same womb, and in one Spirit (see Ephesians 4:4). In taking communion, as we remember that Christ died for us to make us *upright and worthy*, we are to also remember that He bore our sicknesses and carried our pains. This admonition is also to remember to represent Jesus to the rest of the body and to not act unbecomingly. Paul cries,

> Is not the cup of blessing which we bless a sharing in
> the blood of Christ? Is not the bread which we break a
> sharing in the body of Christ? (1 Corinthians 10:16)

Its dual meaning is to remember His body broken for healing. You cannot violate the Lord's command to love one another and expect health. You also cannot ignore what He did for you in bearing your sins, sicknesses and poverty. Communion is about remembering Covenant.

As we examine ourselves, this is not an examination of judgment, but one done in light of the cross wherein we identify with Jesus and see ourselves in Him and in His body. We see that we are to prefer one another in love, being members of one body and also, to remember all that He won for us on through His suffering, death and resurrection that give us victory in life and in the life to come. Paul exclaims. "But thanks be to God, who gives us the victory through our Lord Jesus Christ" (1 Corinthians 15:57). Jesus was specific on what was required of us for this victory. He spoke about His body and blood as true food and drink:

> Jesus therefore said to them, "Truly, truly, I say to you, unless you eat the flesh of the Son of Man and drink His blood, you have no life in yourselves. He who eats My flesh and drinks My blood has eternal life, and I will raise him up on the last day. For My flesh is true food, and My blood is true drink. He who eats My flesh and drinks My blood abides in Me, and I in him. As the living Father sent Me, and I live because of the Father, so he who eats Me, he also shall live because of Me. This is the bread which came down out of heaven; not as the fathers ate, and died, he who eats this bread shall live forever." (John 6:53 58)

God renewed the Covenant that He made with Abraham, giving us a new and better Covenant in the blood of Christ (Hebrews 9:6). The prophets spoke many promises that Christ would fulfill on our behalf. Four essential elements belong to us as we come into the covenant in Christ:

(1) We come into relationship with God though faith in Christ, and enjoy the benefits of the blessings of Abraham. The Holy Spirit points to the way God planned to accomplish our peace with Him and ultimate blessings:

> Moreover, I will give you a new heart and put a new spirit within you; and remove the heart of stone from your flesh and give you a heart of flesh." (Ezekiel 36:26)

God has reconciled us to Himself through Christ. Paul writes to Corinth, "Now all these things are from God, who reconciled us to Himself through Christ" (2 Corinthians 2:18). We enjoy the supreme honor of oneness with Almighty God through Christ. Scripture says, "But the one who unites himself with the Lord is one spirit with Him" (1 Corinthians 6:17). Through Christ, we "become partakers of His divine nature" (2 Peter 1:4). In His great love, Father has chosen to give us new birth by "the Word of truth" (James 1:18).

God brought Abraham into relationship, making Abraham His friend though the Covenant. We are not only friends, but also joint-heirs with Christ (see Romans 8:17). God makes it clear that He wants to dwell with and among us as a Father with His children:

> Or what agreement has the temple of God with idols? For we are the temple of the living God; just as God said, "I WILL DWELL IN THEM AND WALK AMONG THEM; AND I WILL BE THEIR GOD, AND THEY SHALL BE MY PEOPLE."Therefore, COME OUT FROM THEIR MIDST AND BE SEPARATE," says the Lord." AND DO NOT TOUCH WHAT IS UNCLEAN; and I will welcome you. "And I will be a father to you, and you shall be sons and daughters to Me," Says the Lord Almighty. (2 Corinthians 6:16-18)

(2) Health and longevity belonged to Abraham and belongs to us through Christ in our Covenant. We are in Covenant with *Adonai Rapha*, the Lord your Healer! Abraham's health must have been good since He lived one hundred and seventy-five years (Genesis 25:7). Peter restates how we are healed:

> He Himself bore our sins in His body on the cross, so that we might die to sin and live to righteousness; for by His wounds you were healed. For you were continually straying like sheep, but now you have returned to the Shepherd and Guardian of your souls. (1 Peter 2:24-25)

A passage in Isaiah 42 (among others) promised the blessed Messiah:

> I will appoint you as a covenant to the people, as a light to the nations, to open blind eyes, to bring out prisoners from the dungeon, and those who dwell in darkness from the prison. (Isaiah 42:7)

Also, in Isaiah 35 we read,

But He will save you. Then the eyes of the blind will be opened, and the ears of the deaf will be unstopped, then the lame will leap like a deer, and the tongue of the dumb will shout for joy. (Isaiah 35:5-6)

Recall that Jesus stood to read about Himself, quoting a passage from Isaiah 61:

The Spirit of the Lord is upon Me because He has anointed Me to preach the Good News to the poor. He has sent me to proclaim release to the captives, and recovery of sight to the blind, to set free those who are downtrodden and proclaim the favorable year of the Lord. (Luke 4:18-19)

How beautiful Isaiah describes the health and prosperity of God's people by the Holy Spirit:

But there the majestic One, the Lord, shall be for us a place of broad rivers and streams . . . Then the prey of an abundant spoil will be divided; the lame will take the plunder. And no resident will say, "I am sick"; the people who dwell there will be forgiven their iniquity. (Isaiah 33:21, 23-24)

(3) Prosperity is provided in the Covenant. The Bible says that Abraham was very rich in land and cattle. It is said of him, "Now Abram was very rich in livestock, in silver and in gold" (Genesis 13:2). Paul writing to Corinth speaks on sowing and reaping and explains the basis for such riches:

For you know the grace of our Lord Jesus Christ, that though He was rich, yet for your sake He became poor, so that you through His poverty might become rich. (2 Corinthians 8:9)

74

As people consecrated to God, His own possession, we experience not only friendship, but also union with God through Christ, and as His people, He bestows the blessings of His Covenant favor on us, His presence, peace and prosperity.

(4) Our Covenant is an everlasting Covenant for generations— for our descendents. God says, "For I will pour out water on the thirsty land, and streams on the dry ground; I will pour out my Spirit on your offspring, and my blessings on your descendents" (Isaiah 44:3). The promises of God in the Word are for our descendents as well. It is an *everlasting covenant* according the writer of Hebrews,

> May the God of peace, who raised from the dead the great shepherd of the sheep through the blood of the eternal covenant, equip you in every good thing to do His will, working in you that which is pleasing in His sight. (Hebrews 13:20)

Because of confidence in the eternal covenant, we can stand on the Word and pray for our children and grandchildren. When God brought Noah through the flood, He also saved Noah's family. In a similar manner, God commanded one Passover lamb for each family. It shows us the goal for each family to remain whole. The ark was a type of Jesus, who saves us from certain destruction, and will see that our families are brought through as well to safety and blessing. Every promise of God is "Yes" in Christ Jesus. Paul writes,

> Whatever God has promised gets stamped with the Yes of Jesus. In him, this is what we preach and pray, the great Amen, God's Yes and our Yes together, gloriously evident. (2 Corinthians 1:20 MSG)

We can expect to see this fulfilled as we walk by faith. It may take prayer, even fasting, but if we continue to believe the Word, and act on it, we will see our families come safely to the Lord. *Lord, I am ready to dine with You.*

Cleansing and Healing Streams

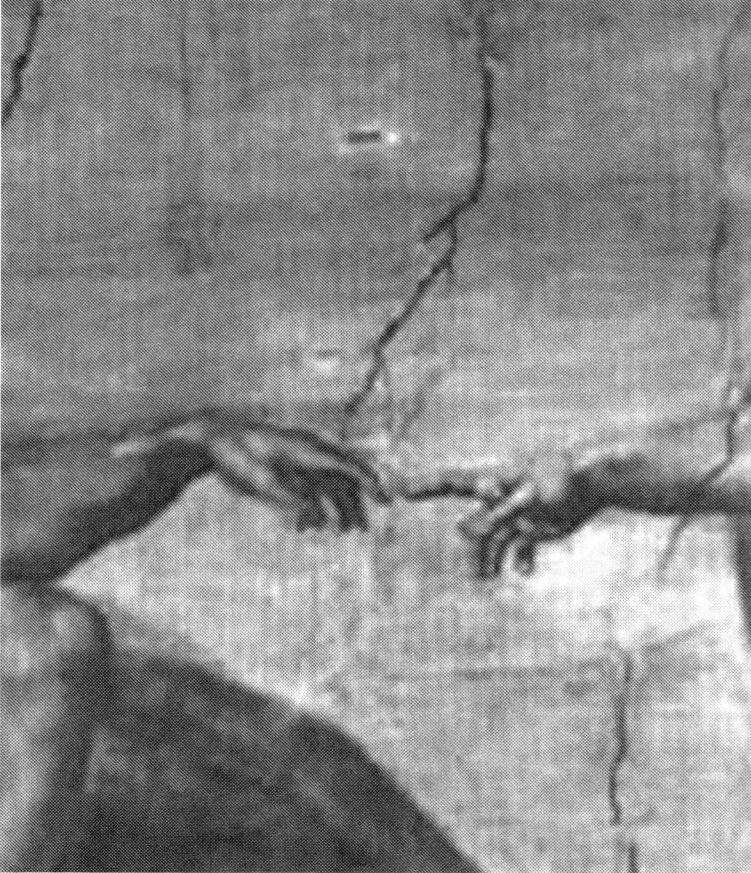

They didn't thirst when he led them through the deserts; he caused the waters to flow out of the rock for them; he split the rock also, and the waters gushed out. (Isaiah 48:21)

CHAPTER NINE

Healing Stream 9

CONFESSION OF THE WORD OF GOD

A very profound truth of the Word of God is often ignored and even ridiculed by many. Confession of the Word of God means a confession of faith. Confession is used in the sense that it means to "profess." It is a profession or a saying of what is believed. Except for receiving healing as one takes communion or during worship, in all the other methods of healing, we see either the sovereignty of God, the gifts of the Spirit, the anointing, laying on of hands, or someone else's faith involved with the healing of an individual. With the believer's confession of the Word that is united with his faith, healing is manifested based on an individual's position of faith in the Word. We should not be bashful about using any of the other means of healing, but we can always experience victory when we apply the Word, using our mouth and our faith.

Faith is expectancy. People assume that to hope is faith, but that kind of hope is not the Bible-kind of hope if it is done by believing something "might" happen. The hope that the Bible speaks of is: faith based on an understanding that one has received what was done through the atonement, and is therefore expecting a manifestation. Much like a pregnant woman expects to give birth and we

Faith is expectancy.

say, "She is expecting," faith anticipates seeing what it believed was already received by faith come into manifestation. Confession is "profession" of the Word, or speaking. Speaking and praying the Word are two different things. Jesus taught His disciples:

> And Jesus answered saying to them, "Have faith in God. Truly I say to you, whoever says to this mountain, 'Be taken up and cast into the sea,' and does not doubt in his heart, but believes that what he says is going to happen, it shall be {granted} him. Therefore I say to you, all things for which you pray and ask,

believe that you have received them, and they shall be {granted} you. And whenever you stand praying, forgive, if you have anything against anyone; so that your Father also who is in heaven may forgive you your transgressions." (Mark 11:22-25).

The first verse of this scripture tells us to have faith in God. The writer of Hebrews shows us faith,

> And without faith it is impossible to please {Him} for he who comes to God must believe that He is, and {that} He is a rewarder of those who seek Him. (Hebrews 11:6)

This explains faith. We believe God exists and will reward us if we seek Him. When we seek Him, we will find Him, and this includes the idea of obedience to Him. A clear demonstration of faith is found in the opening verse of the chapter including the "faith hall of fame" in Hebrews: "Faith is the substance of things hoped for, the evidence of things not seen" (Hebrews 11:1). This means faith is seen as a foundation holding up a structure and a title deed to what is expected. Faith is confident expectation.

We are created in the image of God and His Spirit is within us. We are to imitate Him and speak faith-filled words. When Jesus said, "Follow Me", He was saying, "Follow Me and be My disciple, and I will empower you to be like Me." That was the anticipation of a disciple, to become like His Master.

We literally call into being that which we find promises for in the Word by confessing the Word and exercising our faith. Paul shows us this is what God did in the life of Abraham:

> For this reason {it is} by faith, that {it might be} in accordance with grace, in order that the promise may be certain to all the descendants, not only to those who are of the Law, but also to those who are of the faith of Abraham, who is the father of us all, (as it is written, "A father of many nations have I made you") in the sight of Him whom he believed, {even} God, who

gives life to the dead and calls into being that which does not exist. (Romans 4:16-17)

What a powerful statement; He calls into being that which does not exist. One translation says, "He calls those things that be not as though they are." If God says we were healed by the stripes of Jesus, then we can reach out and call divine health into being. It will be manifested if we stay in faith.

What you say about yourself is so important. Refuse to be called sick or anything but what God says of you. God told Abraham not to call his wife Sarai any longer, but Sarah. He gave her a new name that would reflect what He was calling into being. He also gave Abram a new name, saying,

No longer shall you be called Abram, but your name shall be called Abraham for I shall make you a father of multitude of nations. (Genesis 17:5)

If you are confronted with sickness, call yourself healed. Do not allow any other designation. We are truly made in God's image and likeness, and should act like God—Paul tells us to imitate God (see Ephesians 5:1). The Hebrew letter says, "By faith we understand that the worlds were prepared by the word of God, so that what is seen is was not made out of things which are visible" (Hebrews 11:3). We serve a God who *"gives life to the dead and calls into being that which does not exist."* Use the Word of God, and call into being what God has prepared for you.

The Bible emphasizes that everyone has been given "the measure of faith" (Romans 12:3). We can increase that faith by trusting what the Word of God says and acting on it. Faith that is exercised is a growing faith.

When we speak to a situation according to Mark 11:23, we are addressing the problem (for example, sickness). It says to speak to the mountain and to not doubt. The next verse shows that we pray and believe that we receive, essentially bringing in the answer (healing). To be sure our faith will work, pray and believe we receive, and then to forgive so that we are forgiven—this releases us when we forgive

79

another, and allows our faith to move. This brings confidence when you pray, knowing you have peace with others and peace with God.

Jesus and His disciples come upon a fig tree that Jesus cursed for its lack of fruit. Later, they passed the tree, and Peter comments on the tree being withered.

> And seeing at a distance a fig tree in leaf, He went {to see} if perhaps He would find anything on it; and when He came to it, He found nothing but leaves, for it was not the season for figs. And He answered and said to it, "May no one ever eat fruit from you again!" And His disciples were listening . . . And as they were passing by in the morning, they saw the fig tree withered from the roots {up.} And being reminded, Peter said to Him, "Rabbi, behold, the fig tree which You cursed has withered." (Mark 11:13-14, 11:20, 21)

This story shows the power of words spoken in faith. They have the power to bring life or death. Solomon wrote, "Death and life are in the power of the tongue, and those who love it will eat its fruit" (Proverbs 18:21). Jesus cursed the fig tree, and it withered from the roots up. He did not look back to see if it died. When we curse sickness in the name of Jesus, it is destroyed at its root, which is sin. The supernatural power of the Word spoken in the name of Jesus has gone into effect. Sickness came from the root of sin in the spirit realm, so we curse it in the spirit realm, knowing it has to go. The sick will recover. Expect the manifestation, and thank God for His Word. Just as you may cut off a branch and the leaves are green for a few days, when you curse sickness and pray for healing, the signs or symptoms may disappear immediately, or be seen for a while as your words begin to dry it up from the root.

Sickness and disease is a *manifestation of spiritual death* at work in the body. Mental anguish and torment is a *manifestation of spiritual death* at work in the mind. Yes, emotional problems and mental problems are both a manifestation of spiritual death. Spiritual death means separation from God, who is life. Without life, death works in any area. We need God's life to manifest instead. Since spiritual death is a work of the curse, we need to understand God's remedy—the spirit of life in Christ Jesus (see Romans 8:2). He redeemed us from the curse (see Galatians 3:13).

THE POWER IN THE KINGDOM OF GOD

The Words of your mouth are so important. Review the words that came from Peter's mouth below and Jesus' response to them. The key to moving mountains is contained in them.

> Now when Jesus came into the district of Caesarea Philippi, He {began} asking His disciples, saying, "Who do people say that the Son of Man is?" And they said, "Some {say} John the Baptist; and others, Elijah; but still others, Jeremiah, or one of the prophets." He said to them, "But who do you say that I am?" And Simon Peter answered and said, "Thou art the Christ, the Son of the living God." And Jesus answered and said to him, "Blessed are you, Simon Barjona, because flesh and blood did not reveal {this} to you, but My Father who is in heaven. "And I also say to you that you are Peter, and upon this rock I will build My church; and the gates of Hades shall not overpower it. "I will give you the keys of the kingdom of heaven; and whatever you shall bind on earth shall be bound in heaven, and whatever you shall loose on earth shall be loosed in heaven."
> (Matthew 16:13-19)

Peter's confession that Jesus is the Christ established a foundation for faith. He is the Christ, the Son of the Living God. He is our basis for faith in this life and the life to come. The Greek word for Peter is *petros*, and it means a small rock. The Greek word for rock is *petra* and means a huge mass of rock. Revelation produces faith in us, but with revelation comes responsibility. When Peter received revelation from God, Jesus responded by giving Peter authority (responsibility) to go along with His revelation and faith. Every higher level in faith we obtain begins with revelation.

Peter's confession is a huge founding stone of faith for the church. Some have said this expression means Peter was the founding rock of the church. He was a great apostle after God filled him with the Holy Spirit, but Jesus words reveal something more. Jesus' question was, "*But who do you say that I am?*" The point is that Jesus is the Christ, and this confession of Christ's Deity was inspired by the Holy Spirit. This same confession by us gives us a seat in Christ. When we come into the body of Christ, and our names are written in the Lamb's Book of Life, we are given authority and can exercise this stewardship according to the Word of God. When we speak by the Spirit of God, we establish on Earth the revealed will of God in heavenly places, where we are seated in union with Christ "over all rule and authority and power and dominion, and every name that is named, not only in this age but also in the one to come" (see Ephesians 1:19-21, 2:6).

Jesus tells Peter that He is giving Him the keys to the Kingdom of Heaven. Keys represent authority and stewardship, and Jesus is stating a truth of the Kingdom. We have been given authority, and in the name of Jesus (His Person) we use the words of our mouths to accomplish His Kingdom objectives. We are to help advance the Kingdom of God—His rule, and the movement of Jesus and His followers, which helped to bring it into greater manifestation on earth. Jesus brought a great advance in the movement of God's rule on earth—the Kingdom was His chief message.

The Kingdom of God (and the Kingdom of "Heaven," which is a euphemism for "God") is not a place or unified state such as Israel had under its kings. The Kingdom of God consists of (1) the King, (2) the people of the King, and (3) the Divine force at work within the Kingdom. Thus, the Kingdom includes those who come into the movement of Jesus Christ to bring God's Rule (His absolute rule) to earth by becoming His disciples—obeying His commands and teachings, and continuing His Kingdom work—taking His yoke (see Matthew 11:28-30).

To be under God's rule or reign means to obey God, to walk in His ways—obedient to His covenant. The Divine force within is God's power at work to bring His redemptive purpose to pass in the earth—His saving and healing power. It is manifested in salvation, healing, deliverance and peace (see Luke 11:20).

Concisely, God's rule over His people, the people under His rulership, and the manifestation of His power that brings salvation in all its aspects all constitute the Kingdom. The Kingdom is both within those who believe in God's Son who brought the Kingdom into manifestation, and the future complete manifestation of the kingdom in the millennium (Luke 17:21). The Kingdom is therefore at the same time both a reality that is fulfilled in individuals in the Kingdom, and a reality to be further fulfilled in the future.

The principal of the Kingdom is complete obedience to God. It is the gate of Kingdom living.

The principal of the Kingdom is complete obedience to God. It is the gate of Kingdom living—the commands of the King are absolute. God commands that we should have no god's before Him (see Exodus 20:3). Jesus taught about the characteristics of those in the kingdom primarily in Matthew 5-7. The NIV translation more closely interprets the Kingdom and its movement:

> From the days of John the Baptist until now, the kingdom of heaven has been forcefully advancing, and forceful men lay hold of it. (Matthew 11:12 NIV)

Jesus drew on the Old Testament for His example of the Kingdom's advance. In Micah, the Chief Shepherd (the Breaker) removes stones or obstacles from the sheep pen, which is full and noisy with men, and they burst through behind Him. God speaks through Micah:

> I will surely assemble all of you, Jacob. I will surely gather the remnant of Israel. I will put them together like sheep in the fold; like a flock in the midst of its pasture they will be noisy with men. The breaker goes up before them; they break out, pass through the gate and go out by it. So their king goes on before them. And the LORD at their head. (Micah 2:12-13)

Our authority extends such that in our offensive push to make disciples, as we follow Jesus, the gates of hell will not prevail against the church. We can take them with the words of our mouth. When we speak the Word of God in faith, we are making a withdrawal on the authority in the Word with our mouths. Jesus did this in the wilderness when Satan tempted him. Each time Satan confronted Him with temptation, He said, "It is written . . . or it is also written." The enemy has to flee before the spoken Word of God. It is the sword of the spirit (Ephesians 6:17). We exercise our authority when we say, "By His stripes I was healed." This amounts to telling the enemy, "It is unlawful to hold anyone captive when the Son has set them free" (See John 8:28). The Devil's actions are proven unlawful with your words when you align them with the Word of God. As a disciple, you are essentially acting on what Jesus made available when He bound the strong man and plundered his house. After casting out a devil, Jesus said,

> But no one can enter the strong man's house and plunder his property unless he first binds the strong man, and then he will plunder his house. (Mark 3:27)

We exercise our authority by the words of our mouth. Keys of authority are like the keys to rooms in the Kingdom of Heaven. When you command through your confession, you are using the authority Jesus entrusted to you. He said of our relationship,

> And whatever you ask in My name, that will I do, that the Father may be glorified in the Son. (John 14:13)

The Greek word for ask, in this instance means to demand—not demanding of God, but in essence demanding the situation to change in the name of Jesus. When you use the words of your mouth to speak to the mountain, you have confidence in your authority on Jesus behalf. In the context of our friendship with God, we can expect our requests to be answered when we have spent time with Him and understand His heart. Therefore, when you pray, Jesus said,

> You did not choose Me, but I chose you, and appointed you, that you should go and bear fruit, and {that} your fruit should remain, that whatever you ask of the Father in My name, He may give to you. (John 15:16)

When you ask the Father in the name of Jesus in prayer, God responds. His name is His Person. When you are one spirit with Him, you do not ask amiss. God responds accordingly. Jesus said it in many ways, one later in His same discourse to His friends:

> And in that day you will ask Me no question. Truly, truly, I say to you, if you shall ask the Father for anything, He will give it to you in My name. (John 16:23) (see Section 12, The Power of the Name of Jesus)

When believers lay hands on the sick, it is always in the name of Jesus. I prefer to say, "In the name of Jesus, be healed." We are authorized to command pain and sickness to go, not pray for it to go. With reference to asking for something in prayer that is already made available through Christ, it seemed to me that the Lord said to me one day, "Stop asking me to do what I gave you authority to do." Believers should speak to sickness and demons to flee in the name of Jesus, and not ask the Lord to do what He already gave us authority to do as a part of His kingdom on Earth.

"Stop asking me to do what I gave you authority to do."

Jesus definitely gave believers His authority, His power of attorney here on earth to use His name. Notice Jesus says the believer has this authority because of faith:

> And these signs will accompany those who have believed: in My name they will cast out demons, they will speak with new tongues; they will pick up serpents, and if they drink any deadly {poison,} it shall not hurt them; they will lay hands on the sick, and they will recover. (Mark 16:17-18)

It is in the name of Jesus that believers do the signs. The signs represent the power of God, and the Holy Spirit accompanies us. Jesus also said,

Truly, truly, I say to you, he who believes in Me, the works that I do shall he do also; and greater {works} than these shall he do; because I go to the Father. And whatever you ask in My name, that will I do, that the Father may be glorified in the Son. (John 14:12 13)

The greater works are accomplished as we preach and live the gospel as He commanded. We should have such a sense of His Presence with us, and in us, that it is no problem to speak to situations to line up to the Word, and expect our words to come to pass. This is what it means to act in His name.

Jesus went about doing good and healing all who were oppressed by the devil (see Acts 10:38). Believers do His good works when they impart healing in His name and authority. I do not say that it is not scriptural to ask God to heal the person. It is scriptural to pray for God to heal a person such as in the prayer of faith of James 5. I am stating that as ministers and believers, we have been given authority to represent Jesus to others and use His name, just as He represented the Father on earth and did the works of the Father. In the biblical sense, the name represents the person. The name of Jesus is synonymous with authority.

When cancer is evidenced, I curse the foul disease and command it to go, and lay hands on the person for healing. I frequently thank my Father for the healing because all healing comes from Him.

We have a story of the Lord telling the disciples to cross over to the other side of the Sea of Galilee in the synoptic gospels. Specifically in Matthew, scripture says, "He gave orders to depart to the other side." It was not a suggestion, but a command. Yet the disciples became fearful when the wind and waves grew strong from a storm, and Jesus was sleeping. They woke Him, and He spoke to the storm, rebuking them for their timidity. They forgot the command was to cross the sea, not to go down in it when the circumstances looked bad for them. We can apply this story to our lives. Jesus would say to us today, "I bore your sicknesses and carried your diseases. Do not be afraid. Go on to divine health. Speak to your sickness or pain and be done with it. Do not be timid. Above all, believe you receive. I have empowered you to act like Me."

When Jesus said to the disciples and to us, to follow Him, it carried the meaning of becoming like Him. A student was to strive to be like his master. When we follow Jesus, becoming and making disciples, He empowers us to be like Him. When Peter got out of the boat to go to Jesus who was walking to them on the water, Peter's faith failed, and he sank. He looked at the wind and the waves and became fearful. He was already doing the impossible but became afraid because of the wind and waves—as if he could walk on the water without wind and waves! Jesus did not congratulate Peter on his faith. After all, Peter had gotten out of the boat and walked on the water. No, He asked Peter what happened to his faith! I believe since Peter had committed to follow Jesus and become His disciple, becoming like Him, Jesus wanted Peter to expect to be empowered to do the same things Jesus did—even the impossible.

It must be emphasized here that you will not recover from sickness just because you confess you will be healed, but saying it is so very important. Confession of the Word is highly involved in making healing manifest, but confession is not an end in itself. Confession is as though you set the thermostat for your health, and your health must rise to the level you set. Similarly, your faith will rise to the level of your confession— just as surely as your car will move when you press on the accelerator, your confession will produce eventually produce the necessary faith to overcome. Succinctly, your confession produces faith and eventually results in faith.

When you speak the Word, you are either confessing the Word to increase your knowledge and understanding, to produce faith in your heart, (God writing it in your mind for understanding and on your heart for doing), or you are confessing faith and standing for the manifestation.

Paul wrote to the Corinthians to encourage faith, "to look not at the things that are seen but the things that are unseen" (2 Corinthians 4:18). This indicates expectancy about those unseen things, and a look away from circumstances. Faith is what brings substance to your confession. When confession is mixed with developed faith, the anointing within is activated for healing. Again, confession is agreeing with what God says about circumstances, and not confessing the circumstances and looking to them. It has been said, "Your faith must first move your mouth before it moves you." Before David became the King, he had a number of obstacles to overcome. He told King Saul, "I killed the lion and the bear, and the Lord who saved me from the lion and the bear will save me from this Philistine (1 Samuel 17:36 paraphrase). Then David spoke to the giant that he was to face, rehearsing what he would do to him. Before he ran toward the giant, He called the giant headless! He spoke confidently that the battle is the Lord's, and he would conquer the giant, "and I will kill you and cut off your head" (1 Samuel 17:46). Call your giant dead. Refuse to be called sick. Call yourself saved, healed, delivered and filled.

Those who are healed as they believe and confess the Word are in a position to hold on to their healing more than any other stream of healing. Anyone who receives healing by any means is encouraged to begin to confess their healing. This is boasting in the Lord, telling others who healed you, and how He will heal them too. David sang, "My soul shall make its boast in the Lord" (Psalm 34:2).

Throughout the Epistles of the New Testament we see clearly that we are the Body of Christ. He is the Head and we are the Body. Paul explains,

> And He put all things in subjection under His feet, and gave Him as head over all things to the church, which is His body, the fullness of Him who fills all in all. (Ephesians 1:22-23)

It is not God's will that any part of His body be sick. So whether we are ministering healing or receiving healing, the different streams of healing serve as examples for us. All flows from the Head. Derek Prince called the cross the "Great Stop Sign." On this side of the cross, all the benefits of salvation are available—and the devil must stay on the opposite side as we take our authority. Let your testimony reflect your authority and redemption. John wrote:

> They conquered him by the blood of the lamb and by the word of their testimony, for they did not love their life even in the face of death. (Revelation 12:11)

This stream of healing, confession of the Word, is the one I use most because it is always available to me. Through your spirit, the Holy Spirit will manifest in your life what you say. If you use the Word of God, it will also manifest in your life.

You may need to get forceful with your healing and or deliverance. Do not continue to tolerate something that is robbing you in some way of joy, finances or peace. On a missionary journey, Paul and Barnabus returned to cities in which they had established churches. Luke records,

> The Apostle Paul and Barnabus as they preached in Lystra, Iconium, and Antioch, where they strengthened the believers. They encouraged them to continue in the faith, reminding them that they must enter into the Kingdom of God through many tribulations. (Acts 14:20)

Tribulation, which can mean, pressure, persecution, trouble, affliction and suffering, may come. That is why you need to develop strong faith. The faith life is a lifestyle of overcoming. Unless we overcome, tribulation, trouble, pressure, and burdens will choke the word and prevent it from bearing fruit (see Mark 4:17). Jesus warned us:

> I have told you all this so that you may have peace in me. Here on earth you will have many tribulations. But take heart, because I have overcome the world. (John 16:33)

Be aggressive about healing and deliverance. Get free and stay free.

God and His Word are One

You can "stand" on the Word of God, meaning that you can refuse to budge from what the Word of God says about your situation. God and His Word are One. His Word is a part of Himself. Because God is One, He cannot be separated from His Word. In the same way, Jesus and His name are One. The name is the person. This is easy to understand because you cannot be separated from your word. Your word reveals who you are. Just as your word and the keeping of such identifies your character, the character of God and of Jesus Christ are behind the Word of God. God is truth and the Bible teaches, "It is impossible for God to lie" (Hebrews 6:18). God also watches over His Word to perform it (see Jeremiah 1:12). As the Word of God (see John 1:1), Jesus only spoke the Word of the Father. The Word of God is "God breathed," so when you read or speak the Word, you are speaking words backed up by the character of God. You rely on the trustworthiness of the One who spoke it. Jesus describes how powerful His words are: "The words that I have spoken to you are Spirit and are Life" (John 6:63).

Take a position of faith in the Word. It is faith in God. Receive the Word of God for what it is, not the word of a man but "the Word of God, which performs its work in you because you believe" (see 1 Thessalonians 2:13). *Lord, Your Spirit is upon me and in me, and Your Words are in my mouth. They will not depart from the mouth of my offsprings, or my offsprings' offsprings (see Isaiah 59:21).*

CHAPTER TEN

Cleansing and Healing Stream 10

DELIVERANCE & HEALING

The ministry of Jesus included deliverance from demonic oppression, and demonic possession. Some whom Jesus encountered were possessed, meaning a demon was in control of the person, and some were demonized, meaning they had a demon in them but still appeared normal, but with certain limitations, including infirmity. Many times the Bible says that He cast out demons, some of which were related to disease or physical oppression. Man has tried to take the Word of God on this issue and conform it to fit a more "modern" way of thinking or experience. It has been said that primitive belief was that the disease was a demon, but modern science has shown us the causes are not demonic. To this I say, the Bible is "God breathed" (see 2 Timothy 2:16) and does not need man's rationalization. Where the Bibles says that Jesus cast out a demon, He did. I count at least fourteen instances in the gospels where Jesus delivered people from demonic spirits.

Jesus often rebuked the disciples for their lack of faith. For three and one-half years they lived around Him, and they saw His miracles and still had little faith while He was alive. Lest we major in faith at the expense of those who believe they have little, a story in Mark demonstrates Jesus' compassion for one who lacked faith. A man came to Jesus to heal his demonized son. The man had first sought help from the disciples, but they had been unable to cast out the demon. Mark explains,

> And one of the crowd answered Him, "Teacher, I brought You my son, possessed with a spirit which makes him mute; and whenever it seizes him, it slams him to the ground and he foams at the mouth, and grinds his teeth and stiffens out. I told Your disciples to cast it out, and they could not do it." And He answered them and said, "O unbelieving generation, how long

91

shall I be with you? How long shall I put up with you? Bring him to Me!" They brought the boy to Him. When he saw Him, immediately the spirit threw him into a convulsion, and falling to the ground, he began rolling around and foaming at the mouth. (Mark 9:17-20)

Notice the boy was mute all the time, but occasionally had episodes of greater demon control. The man had asked if Jesus could do anything. Mark writes,

And Jesus said to him, "If You can! All things are possible to him who believes." Immediately the boy's father cried out and {began} saying, "I do believe; help my unbelief." (Mark 9:23-24)

The boy's father admitted having small faith and asked for help to have more. He believed in his heart but his mind was not yet in agreement. Only the Word of God can renew our minds and reconcile mind and heart issues (see Romans 12:2, Hebrews 4:12). Jesus did not tell the man to return when he had more faith for his son's deliverance. No. Jesus cast out the demon; Jesus' compassion bridged the distance in the faith needed and the faith possessed. Keep in mind, the disciples had already been given authority to cast out devils in the name of Jesus, but lacked the faith necessary to deal with this kind of demon. Luke shows us their excitement at their authority, "And the seventy returned again with joy, saying, Lord, even the demons are subject to us through Your name" (Luke 10:17 MKJV). Jesus clarified that prayer was necessary for this particular type of demon, and Matthew's account adds that fasting may be necessary (see Matthew 17:21).

The book of Acts also shows deliverance from demonic spirits, such as when Paul cast the spirit of divination out of a servant girl. The girl had been making a profit for her master by fortune telling. Luke gives us details of the event:

Following after Paul and us, she kept crying out, saying, "These men are bond-servants of the Most High God, who are proclaiming to you the way of salvation."

She continued doing this for many days. But Paul was greatly annoyed, and turned and said to the spirit, "I command you in the name of Jesus Christ to come out of her!" And it came out at that very moment. (Acts 16:17-18)

Paul must have not cast the demon out of her earlier in order to give the girl time to become a believer. Otherwise, something worse might come on her after Paul cast the demonic spirit out. Jesus warned,

When the unclean spirit has gone out of a man, he walks through dry places seeking rest. And finding none, he says, I will return to my house from which I came out. And when he comes, he finds *it* swept and decorated. And he goes and takes seven other spirits more wicked than himself, and entering in, they dwell there. And the last state of that man is worse than the first. (Luke 11:24-26 MKJV)

Paul obviously felt it was time to deal with it, and spoke to the spirit, "I command you in the name of Jesus Christ to come out of her!" Paul used his authority to command the evil spirit to go, just as Jesus said all believers should do (see Mark 16:17, Matthew 10:2).

Any operation of the supernatural in knowing or predicting the future always stems from one of two sources, God or demonic spirits. The "word of wisdom" is a gift of the Spirit, in which the Spirit of God gives a word on the future for someone in the Body of Christ (see 1 Corinthians 12). The Holy Spirit also speaks of things to come to believers directly (see John 16:13). The servant girl has a spirit of divination—not one from God.

Jesus casted out evil spirits and commanded his followers to do the same. Some are aware of intrusions by demonic spirits because the spirits have manifested overtly. Others are completely unaware that some of their actions and illnesses are from demonic sources. Lastly, some do not want to be aware of such—they are fellowshipping with something that they want to keep.

The biblical accounts do not provide us with all the details of each deliverance Jesus performed, or the disciples for that matter, as to the time it took or the complete manifestation. When Jesus set free the demonized man in the Country of the Gerasenes, the verb tense indicates that Jesus had been saying to him more than once, "Come out of the man, you unclean spirit!" (Mark 5:8). The demons recognized Jesus' authority and knew they would have to obey—but the man had a legion of demons. Jesus allowed the demons to enter swine; it would appear, to save the man physical trauma when the legion of demons left him.

Jesus is the bread of life. He is healing, deliverance and His blood reconciles us to God and imparts righteousness to us. Healing and deliverance is a part of our inheritance through the Atonement of Christ Jesus. In the following account, when a woman came to Jesus, He told her that what she asked was "the children's bread." Since Jesus said, "I am the bread of life," we see that He gave up His body for our health and deliverance. Mark tells the story:

> But after hearing of Him, a woman whose little daughter had an unclean spirit, immediately came and fell at His feet. Now the woman was a Gentile, of the Syrophenician race. And she kept asking Him to cast the demon out of her daughter. And He was saying to her, "Let the children be satisfied first, for it is not good to take the children's bread and throw it to the dogs." But she answered and said to Him, "Yes, Lord, {but} even the dogs under the table feed on the children's crumbs." And He said to her, "Because of this answer go your way; the demon has gone out of your daughter." And going back to her home, she found the child lying on the bed, the demon having departed. (Mark 7:25 30)

Jesus explained that God sent Him first to the Jews who, being children of Abraham, had a Covenant. However, the woman's faith and persistence won favor. He said the demon left her daughter. To us, Jesus would say, "You have a Covenant. You are children of Abraham because you are of faith (see Galatians 3:7). You are kept in the Blood of the Eternal Covenant (see Hebrews 13:20). Therefore, receive the children's bread, and be delivered and healed."

While avoiding the debate on whether believers can have a demonic spirit (not complete possession but demonized), I candidly say, something of this nature has been observed in believers. Many who love the Lord and serve Him, have to deal with generational spirits, and spirits who intrude through the open demonic gates of disobedience, unforgiveness, traumas, inner vows and judgments, curses (ancestral curses, occult activity, idolatry, unlawful sexual unions, lying, etc.). They may eventually have "head on" encounters with the demonic realm and then seek help. Or, I am concerned, they may be diagnosed wrongly with a mental illness because they begin experiencing supernatural occurrences; e.g., hearing voices or seeing visions that are not from God.

People who have dabbled in New Age encounters, witchcraft, eastern mysticism, or illicit sex are especially vulnerable to demonic spirits, as are victims of abuse. It is not uncommon for people to talk about the spirit of fear, yet not with the understanding that the spirit of fear is an entity, not just a feeling. Definitely, God has not given us a spirit of fear, but a spirit of power, love, and a sound mind (2 Timothy 1:7). Any spirit of fear is of the enemy.

Jesus used the power of rebuke, and we should also. He rebuked demons, and they left people. He rebuked a fever in Peter's mother-in-law, which suggests to me that the fever was from a demon. To rebuke means to charge, admonish, forbid, or strictly, to judge from a higher position, even to mock or laugh. That is what we do when we rebuke a demonic spirit in the name of Jesus, and command in the name of Jesus, or curse sickness in the name of Jesus. We are taking authority from a higher position of authority, our position as children of God and as joint-heirs with Christ. We have authority in the name of Jesus. Again, the name represents the person. It is the same as if Jesus were present. When we speak by the Spirit of God, God is speaking through us! Demons have to obey.

Jesus used the power of rebuke, and we should also.

All believers have authority and power in the name of Jesus to cast out demons (Mark 16, Matthew 10:1, Luke 9:1, and 10:17). However, God has called a number of ministries to specifically help people get free from evil spirits. A part of Jesus' platform of ministry that He put forth was to "proclaim release to the captives and to set at liberty the oppressed" (Luke 4:18).

It grieves me to observe people carrying shame, guilt, anger, or something from the trauma of abuse or ancestral spirits that limits them and prevents fullness of joy. Deliverance has not been the primary focus of my ministry, but I have been used of God in a few cases to set at liberty the oppressed both in public ministry sessions and in private sessions for more complete freedom from all captivity and/or oppression by the enemy. Jesus came to destroy the works of the enemy, and this is also our mission as believers (see 1 John 3:8).

Jesus came to destroy the works of the enemy, and this is also our mission as believers.

When one repeatedly acts in a way that brings guilt and shame, and feels powerless to be free of it, or is tormented in some way, God has an answer. Such persons might need ministry to free them from the oppression and bondage. *Lord, You are my Deliverer.* Since everything we receive is through the cross, let your testimony reflect your authority and redemption. Remember we always triumph, we always overcome. John wrote:

> They conquered him by the blood of the lamb and by
> the word of their testimony, for they did not love their
> life even in the face of death. (Revelation 12:11)

You are invited to pray this prayer of deliverance, cleansing and healing:

Father, I thank you for Your great mercy. I forgive everyone who ever hurt me. I see their sins on the cross, and I forgive them. I thank you for forgiving me. I forgive myself for hurting others and failing You. Father, I thank you for salvation through Your Son, Jesus Christ—I receive the sprinkling of the blood of Christ, and desire to walk in obedience to Him. In union with Him, I command any evil spirit or evil presence that took advantage of my wounds or sins to leave in Jesus Christ's name. I thank You Father for perfect freedom. I receive my cleansing, healing, deliverance and freedom in Christ Jesus' precious name. Amen

CHAPTER ELEVEN

Healing Stream 11

PRAISE AND WORSHIP

The Great redemptive Chapter in Isaiah 53 paints a vivid and concrete picture of the totality of redemption. God put the sin of the world on Jesus—He literally became sin for us (see 2 Corinthians 5:21). He also became sickness for us. Isaiah prophesies:

> Surely He has borne our griefs (sicknesses, weaknesses, and distresses) and carried our sorrows and pains [of punishment], yet we [ignorantly] considered Him stricken, smitten, and afflicted by God [as if with leprosy]. Yet it was the will of the Lord to bruise Him; he has put Him to grief and made Him sick (Isaiah 53:4, 10 AMP).

We were in Adam when sin entered the world, and we inherited his fallen nature. Since the root of sickness is sin, which entered through the fall of man, God had to put it all on the Lord, and redemption provided to us to put us in the Second Adam, Jesus Christ. Sickness qualifies as incipient death (see Romans 5:15). While it may not always result in death, many times it does, or makes some wish they were dead! God made Jesus to become a sin offering and defeat sickness for us. Therefore, we would be foolish to keep what He already has dealt with for us.

We were reconciled to God through Christ, and abide in Him, so God now sees us in Christ. Since Christ became a sin offering for us, God now sees us in Him as healed and righteous. Paul writes to Corinth,

> God made this sinless man be a sin offering on our behalf, so that in union with Him we might fully share in God's righteousness. (2 Corinthians 5:21 JNT)

Peter also gives us a verse worthy of meditation:

> He himself bore our sins in his body on the stake, so that we might die to sins and live for righteouness—by his wounds you were healed. (1 Peter 2:24 JNT)

Knowing that we were healed by His stripes, in gratitude for His goodness, let us thank God for what He blessed us with in redemption, and praise Him for our health, refusing to allow anything to remain that is not of God. Again, thank and praise Him for freedom from the power of sin and freedom from all sickness. Do not stop until your body lines up with the Truth.

Thank and praise Him for freedom from the power of sin and freedom from all sickness.

Because of God's great mercy, He placed us in Christ when He conquered sin, sickness and the enemy through Christ. It is a cause for exaltation. Paul exclaims, "God disarmed the principalities and powers that were ranged against us and made a public display of them, having triumphed over them through Christ" (Colossians 2:15). This is truly Good News. We have Christ in us and manifesting through us a great triumph. Writes Paul,

> But thanks be to God, Who in Christ always leads us in triumph [as trophies of Christ's victory] and through us spreads and makes evident the fragrance of the knowledge of God everywhere. (2 Corinthians 2:14-15 AMP)

As sweet perfume unto God, Through Christ, "Let us constantly offer up a sacrifice of praise to God, the fruit of our lips giving thanks and glory to His name" (Hebrews 13:15). Let us worship Him in spirit and truth as true worshippers whom God is seeking after (see John 4:23).

Praise and worship are powerful means to draw closer to God. In worship, His very presence sometimes is in manifestation. A worshipper writes, "He inhabits the praises of His people" (Psalm 22:3). Time spent in worship, prayer and meditation on the Word, bring you into direct contact with Deity. Healing manifests as a natural outflow of being in His Presence. Yes, He lives in us and is present at all times but on occasion, manifests His presence in a greater measure. James encourages, "Draw near to God and He will draw near to you" (James 4:8).

You may perhaps become aware of His subtle fragrance filling the room as you seek Him in worship or meditation on His Word, and sometimes He begins to speak to you. Pain and sickness will disappear without your having consciously become aware of when it left—because you are so in awe of God's special manifestation.

Praise ceases the enemy. David praised, "You have taught children and nursing infants to give you praise. They silence your enemies who were seeking revenge" (Psalm 8:2). Praise and worship are powerful means to bring healing to your heart, soul, emotions and body. Create a new atmosphere around you with a new level of praise. When you get into high praise, it is as though you are turning up the thermostat. At certain levels, bacteria cannot live, nor can serpents. Go higher. Consider your sickness in one hand, and your praise in the other. As you fill up one, the other will go higher. If you are focusing on the sickness, it gets heavier. But when you focus on praise and worship, it gets heavier and the sickness lifts right off. Live praising vertically, and it will help you live horizontally. By this I mean, keep your eyes on the Master, not on the circumstances. Magnify Him and not the circumstances.

A King Uses Mighty Weapons
Against the Enemy

Praise was a mighty weapon in the days of the kings of Israel and is a mighty weapon today. When King Jehoshaphat was ruling in Judah (the southern tribes of Israel), three kings brought their armies against Judah. The Bible describes the armies as "a great multitude." Jehoshaphat's response to the invasion is a wonderful example for us to follow when our circumstances appear overwhelming. In the midst of trials, temptations, sickness, or lack, follow this example of faith:

1. "Seek first the His kingdom and His righteousness; and all these things will be added unto you" (Matthew 6:33). Seeking first the kingdom is essentially seeking God's Kingdom, His rule. The kingdom is a spiritual reality, but it is also governed by principles

99

that Jesus gave us during His ministry on earth. Therefore, the first thing to do is seek God. Jehoshaphat did this. God is the only source when the situation is hopeless from a human standpoint. Jehoshaphat set his face toward God, the source of all, "And Jehoshaphat was afraid and turned his attention to the Lord" (2 Chronicles 20:3).

2. Bring out a powerful weapon from your spiritual arsenal—fasting and prayer. Jehoshaphat "proclaimed a fast throughout all Judah" (2 Chronicles 20:3). The enemy is demoralized when he encounters a believer who fasts and prays; how much more, when an entire nation fasts! Spiritual power is prominent in the midst of a fast. Our spirits begin to take ascendancy over the natural. Greater sensitivity to God is the result, and hearing and following God take precedence. When believers set themselves to seek God more than their necessary food—I believe He is pleased and responds. Job exclaimed, "I have not departed from the command of His lips; I have treasured the words of His mouth more than my necessary food" (Job 23:12).

3. Put on the garment of praise (see Isaiah 61:3). Praise is something you put on. Jehoshaphat put on this garment:

> And he said, "O LORD, the God of our fathers, are You not God in the heavens? And are You not ruler over all the kingdoms of the nations? Power and might are in Your hand so that no one can stand against You." (2 Chronicles 20:6)

I am reminded of how King David praised the Lord in a similar manner:

> So David blessed the LORD in the sight of all the assembly; and David said, "Blessed are You, O LORD God of Israel our father, forever and ever. Yours, O LORD, is the greatness and the power and the glory and the victory and the majesty, indeed everything that is in the heavens and the earth is Yours; Yours is the

100

dominion, O LORD, and You exalt Yourself as head over all. Both riches and honor come from You, and You rule over all, and in Your hand is power and might; and it lies in Your hand to make great and to strengthen everyone. Now therefore, our God, we thank You, and praise Your glorious name." (1 Chronicles 29:10-13)

Jehoshaphat praised God for who He is; and then Jehoshaphat rehearsed God's faithfulness. He said:

Did You not, O our God, drive out the inhabitants of this land before Your people Israel and give it to the descendants of Abraham Your friend forever? They have lived in it, and have built You a sanctuary there for Your name, saying, 'Should evil come upon us, the sword, or judgment, or pestilence, or famine, we will stand before this house and before You (for Your name is in this house) and cry to You in our distress, and You will hear and deliver us. ((2 Chronicles 20:7-9))

4. Do not waiver once you start to seek God. Our gaze is Heavenward. Keep your face set toward Him in total dependence, and cry out to Him as Jehoshaphat did for his people:

O our God, will You not judge them? For we are powerless before this great multitude who are coming against us; nor do we know what to do, but our eyes are on You. (2 Chronicles 20:12)

5. When God answers, continue to proclaim trust in Him and His Word. This includes a Word that may come through a prophet, such as Jahaziel:

Then in the midst of the assembly the Spirit of the LORD came upon Jahaziel the son of Zechariah, the son of Benaiah, the son of Jeiel, the son of Mattaniah, the Levite of the sons of Asaph; and he said, "Listen, all Judah and the inhabitants of Jerusalem and King

Jehoshaphat: thus says the LORD to you, 'Do not fear or be dismayed because of this great multitude, for the battle is not yours but God's. Tomorrow go down against them. Behold, they will come up by the ascent of Ziz, and you will find them at the end of the valley in front of the wilderness of Jeruel. You need not fight in this battle; station yourselves, stand and see the salvation of the LORD on your behalf, O Judah and Jerusalem. Do not fear or be dismayed; tomorrow go out to face them, for the LORD is with you." (2 Chronicles 20:15-17)

6. Do not fear. In the passages above, God told the people twice to not fear or be dismayed. Fear paralyzes, but faith empowers. Another word for empower is authorize. When God speaks to empower, He is also giving authority over the situation.

7. The battle is not yours. Every battle has a spiritual reality as well as a natural reality. God is Spirit. Identify with your spiritual source in prayer and fasting, then allow God to fight for you: Isaiah proclaims, "I will contend with the one who contend with you" (Isaiah 49:25b). He also writes, "No weapon formed against you will prosper" (Isaiah 54:17).

8. Worship, Worship, Worship. See this worship of gratitude in Israel,

> Jehoshaphat bowed his head with his face to the ground, and all Judah and the inhabitants of Jerusalem fell down before the LORD, worshiping the LORD. (2 Chronicles 20:18)

It has been said, "You may experience God's presence in praise, but you find His miracles in worship."

9. Praise God without inhibition. Praise loudly and passionately. The Levites used this weapon mightily:

The Levites, from the sons of the Kohathites and of the sons of the Korahites, stood up to praise the LORD God of Israel, with a very loud voice. (2 Chronicles 20:19)

10. Unconditional trust is a guarantee of salvation and deliverance. Security and success is available when you trust in the Lord. The Prophet advised:

> Put your trust in God and you will be established. Put your trust in His prophets and you will succeed. (2 Chronicles 20:20)

11. Put on your heavenly clothing, and put praise in your mouth. Face the situation in the full armor of God (see Ephesians 6:11). You will have put on Christ (see Romans 14:14), the armor of light (Romans 14:12), and be going forward in holy attire with praise in your mouth:

> He appointed those who sang to the LORD and those who praised Him in holy attire, as they went out before the army and said, "Give thanks to the LORD, for His lovingkindness is everlasting," (2 Chronicles 20:21)

12. Expect victory. If you are expecting, then you are in faith. If you are merely hoping, then turn up your level of faith, and believe for triumph. God goes before you as He did with the early disciples. Writes Paul,

> But thanks be to God, Who in Christ always leads us in triumph [as trophies of Christ's victory] and through us spreads and makes evident the fragrance of the knowledge of God everywhere. (2 Corinthians 2:14-15 AMP)

Picture yourself in a mighty Roman Triumphe such as the Romans put on after a conquest. They paraded the spoils of war and the captives through the streets of Rome. They and all of Rome reveled in their conquest. They celebrated with sacrifices, music, dancing, and all came out to see the mighty triumphe. Some conquerors rode in with elephants or lions pulling their chariots and their captives and booty trailing them. The incense they offered to their so-called gods is nothing in comparison to the sweet fragrance of Christ through us to God as we spread the knowledge of Him every place we go.

13. Praise ceases the enemy, and to the victors go the spoils!

> Then they began singing and praising, the LORD set ambushes against the sons of Ammon, Moab and Mount Seir, who had come against Judah; so they were routed. For the sons of Ammon and Moab rose up against the inhabitants of Mount Seir destroying them completely; and when they had finished with the inhabitants of Seir, they helped to destroy one another. When Judah came to the lookout of the wilderness, they looked toward the multitude, and behold, they were corpses lying on the ground, and no one had escaped. When Jehoshaphat and his people came to take their spoil, they found much among them, including goods, garments and valuable things which they took for themselves, more than they could carry. And they were three days taking the spoil because there was so much. (2 Chronicles 20:22-25)

14. Remember to thank and praise God for the victory in the midst of the triumph. Jehoshaphat and his people did a good job of it.

> They came to Jerusalem with harps, lyres and trumpets to the house of the LORD. And the dread of God was on all the kingdoms of the lands when they heard that the LORD had fought against the enemies of Israel. (2 Chronicles 20:28-29)

God Enjoys Praise and Responds

This section would not be complete without the New Testament example of praise in one of the darkest hours for two followers of Christ. The authorities took Paul and Silas to the head magistrate after they cast a demon out of a servant girl, who had been bringing her masters profit telling fortunes. In this particular case, while Paul and Silas were preaching and teaching in Philippi, they did not experience much persecution. But when they caused a stir by casting out the demon, resulting in the loss of future gain from fortune telling, the enemy stirred up people to stop them.

Without even the hint of a trial, the magistrates stripped and beat Paul and Silas with rods. As if it were not enough to beat them, they conducted the beating in public without their robes.

In this particular type of beating, the tormentor hoisted the victim in the air and beat him on his feet with the intent to maim and cripple. It could have also taken place on other parts of their body. Then they put Paul and Silas' bleeding and wounded feet in stocks in the inner prison, in other words, in the darkest dungeon. But Paul and Silas had a different spirit and responded with praise. Luke records:

Paul and Silas had a different spirit and responded with praise.

> But about midnight Paul and Silas were praying and singing hymns of praise to God, and the prisoners were listening to them (Acts 16:25).

In the darkest part of the night, Paul and Silas sang hymns of praise so loudly the other prisoners heard them! Their praises caught the interest of God:

> And suddenly there came a great earthquake, so that the foundations of the prison house were shaken; and immediately all the doors were opened and everyone's chains were unfastened. (Acts 16:26)

Do not be slack in praise and worship. It moves the heavens. And your benefits are great. You can use the Psalms, which are songs. We lose the full impact by just reading them. David sang to the Lord:

> How blessed is he who considers the helpless; the Lord will deliver him in a day of trouble. The Lord will protect him, and keep him alive, and he shall be called blessed upon the earth; The Lord will sustain him upon his sickbed; in his illness, thou dost restore him to health. (Psalm 41:1, 2, 4)

> Bless the LORD, O my soul, And all that is within me, bless His holy name. Bless the LORD, O my soul, And forget none of His benefits; Who pardons all your iniquities, Who heals all your diseases; Who redeems your life from the pit, Who crowns you with lovingkindness and compassion; Who satisfies your years with good things, So that your youth is renewed like the eagle. (Psalm 103:1-5)

As you still your thoughts on sickness or circumstances and lift your heart in worship, magnifying the Lord, your problems seem less significant and eventually are outshined by His glory. Often they diminish until they are gone entirely. David sang,

> I would have despaired unless I had believed that I would see the goodness of the Lord in the land of the living. Wait for the Lord; be strong and let your heart take courage; yes, wait for the Lord. (Psalm 27:13-14)

See the beauty and peace of worship in this Psalm:

> The Lord is my strength and my shield; my heart trusts in Him and I am helped; therefore my heart exults, and with my song I shall thank Him. The Lord is their strength and He is a saving defense to His anointed. (Psalm 28:7-8)

We have a Psalm preserved for us that runs the gamut of praise, worship, thanksgiving, a plea for help, and a confident praise in God's goodness. This Psalm is a comfort and encouragement. The Psalmist records:

> I shall bless the Lord at all times; His praise shall continually be in my mouth. My soul shall make its boast in the Lord; the humble shall hear it and rejoice. O magnify the Lord with me; and let us exalt His name together. I sought the Lord and He answered me, and delivered me from all my fears. They looked to Him and were radiant, and their faces shall never be ashamed. The poor man cried and the Lord heard him, and saved him out of all his troubles. The angel of the Lord encamps about those who fear Him and rescues them. O taste and see that the Lord is good; How blessed is the man who takes refuge in Him (O the joy of those who trust in Him). O fear the Lord, you His saints; for to those who fear Him, there is no want; the young lions do lack and suffer hunger; but they who seek the Lord shall not be in want of any good thing. Many are the afflictions of the righteous but the Lord delivers him out of them all.
> (Psalm 34:1-10, 19)

The poor man cried and the Lord heard him, and saved him out of all his troubles

How blessed we are to have the Psalms to help us focus on the Lord, magnify Him, and sing His praises. David also penned,

> You will make known to me the path of life; In Your presence is fullness of joy; in Your right hand there are pleasures forever." (Psalm 16:11).

I personally experienced healing during worship from a source of pain that was recurrent. A certain situation always triggered a sense of rejection. After one such incident, I sat at my piano and began to play and sing, magnifying the Lord and praising Him for how He always caused me to triumph. The deep emotional pain left and never returned. It was both a healing and a maturing at the same time. Stop now and allow gratitude for His kindness to move you to worship. He is worthy of praise. *Lord, I will praise you forever and ever!*

Cleansing and Healing Streams

They didn't thirst when he led them through the deserts; he caused the waters to flow out of the rock for them; he split the rock also, and the waters gushed out. (Isaiah 48:21)

CHAPTER TWELVE

Healing Stream 12

ANGELIC ACTIVITY

Angels are active in performing God's desires, even as it pertains to healing. Jacob saw their activity coming and going from the throne of God. Jacob named the place Bethel, meaning "house of God." The Bible says:

> He had a dream, and behold, a ladder was set on the earth with its top reaching to heaven; and behold, the angels of God were ascending and descending on it. (Genesis 28:12)

Jesus also experienced angelic assistance and spoke of angels. He said to religious leaders:

> Verily, verily, I say unto you that hereafter you shall see the heavens opened and the angels of God ascending and descending upon the Son of Man. (John 1:51)

I believe Jesus said this to indicate that He is now the house of God, indwelled by the fullness of Deity (see Colossians 2:9). We should expect the same experience since we are indwelled by the Holy Spirit.

The writer of Hebrews penned one of the best descriptions of angels. He writes,

> Are they not all ministering spirits, sent out to render service for the sake of those who will inherit salvation? (Hebrews 1:14)

This comes on the heels of one of the Psalms, which describes angels and how they respond:

Bless the LORD, you His angels, Mighty in strength, who perform His word, Obeying the voice of His word! Bless the LORD, all you His hosts, You who serve Him, doing His will. (Psalm 103:20-21)

Since angels respond to the voice of God, His Word, give God these same praise words to use on your behalf by the angels.

In the book by the same name, Daniel speaks in the first person:

> And behold, one who resembled a human being was touching my lips; then I opened my mouth and spoke and said to him who was standing before me, "O my lord, as a result of the vision anguish has come upon me, and I have retained no strength. For how can such a servant of my lord talk with such as my lord? As for me, there remains just now no strength in me, nor has any breath been left in me." Then this one with human appearance touched me again and strengthened me. He said, "O man of high esteem, do not be afraid. Peace be with you; take courage and be courageous!" Now as soon as he spoke to me, I received strength and said, "May my lord speak, for you have strengthened me." (Daniel 10:16-19)

An angel came and ministered to Daniel after he became weak due to the vision he experienced. The angle strengthened Daniel by touching him and speaking to him!

We also see angelic activity to strengthen Elijah the prophet, who was in great depression brought on by fear and exhaustion. This angel also provided food for Elijah as well as supernatural strength that lasted Elijah forty days!

> He lay down and slept under a juniper tree; and behold, there was an angel touching him, and he said to him, "Arise, eat." Then he looked and behold, there was at his head a bread cake baked on hot stones, and a jar of water. So he ate and drank and lay down again. The

110

angel of the LORD came again a second time and touched him and said, "Arise, eat, because the journey is too great for you." So he arose and ate and drank, and went in the strength of that food forty days and forty nights to Horeb, the mountain of God. (1 Kings 19: 5-8)

An angel ministered to our Lord Jesus in the wilderness after His forty-day fast and temptation by Satan, and again in the garden of Gethsemane (see Matthew 4:11, Luke 22:43). He was weak from hunger in the wilderness, and He sweat great drops of blood in prayer in Gethsemane. In both instances, He received strength from angels to continue. Before His crucifixion, Jesus, declared His authority to call on twelve legions of angels, if He so chose (see Matthew 26:53). I find that Jesus spoke often of angels and their activities. He explained angels would be active in the end-times events at His return, angels rejoiced at one salvation, and yet God limited their knowledge of some things. Jesus said that little children have angels that are constantly before God:

See that you do not despise one of these little ones, for I say to you that their angels in heaven continually see the face of My Father who is in heaven. (Matthew 18:10)

The ministry of angels is a part of God's order in creation. We are in no way inferior to the angels, but we are limited due to the nature of our natural bodies. They operate in the spiritual realm in their assignment to minister to and for us. They are very strong, and yet obey the Word. I believe that we each have an angel or angels assigned to us, according to what God has assigned us to accomplish on earth.

Similar to what is recorded in Bible days, in this age, angels have been observed in church services, and in private visitations, just as they appeared in the New Testament to help the saints. They have sometimes been reported to have touched a person and delivered God's healing Word. They are sent to minister to us, and in doing so, sometimes intervene in our lives to protect us from disaster. On

111

shipboard, an angel brought word to Paul that all on board the ship would be saved (see Acts 27). Two angels rescued Lot and his family from Sodom before God sent judgment on the city (see Genesis 19). Also, an angel rescued Peter from prison (see Acts 12).

Angels are ministering to us in many ways unobserved. The Bible tells us to take heart if we fear the Lord, because angels protect us and rescue us: "The Angel of the Lord encamps about those who fear Him, and rescues them" (Psalms 34:7). They are acting in obedience to God's orders! Another wonderful Psalm tells us, "For He will give His angels charge concerning you, to guard you in all your ways." (Psalm 91:11). As we pray, God releases angels on our behalf. The Prophet Elisha bears witness to this protection. He asked the Lord to open the eyes of his servant to see the greater number of angels with them than with their aggressors. The Bible account says:

> "Do not fear, for those who are with us are more than those who are with them." Then Elisha prayed and said, "O LORD, I pray, open his eyes that he may see " And the LORD opened the servant's eyes and he saw; and behold, the mountain was full of horses and chariots of fire all around Elisha. (2 Kings 6:16-17)

Be aware, some may also encounter malevolent spirits by attempting great things for God. God grants discernment. Thank God for our angels who "guard us in all our ways."

> For He will give His angels orders concerning you, to protect you in all your ways. They will support you with their hands so that you will not strike your foot against a stone. (Psalm 91:11 –12 HCSB)

Be encouraged in your healing. God has many streams of healing from which you may receive healing. Acknowledge His goodness and provision, and expect His best. Remember and think on God's goodness. David writes, "The Lord is good and He does good" (Psalm 119:68). James brags on God's constancy and goodness. Writes James,

He will give His angels orders concerning you, to protect you in all your ways

112

Every good thing given and every perfect gift is from above, coming down from the Father of lights, with whom there is no variation or shifting shadow."(James 1:17).

I am not suggesting that you to rely on angels. No, rely on the Word of God. I have merely given you examples of different streams of God's healing, of which angels may play a part at times. *Lord, thank you for the angels You send to guard and minister to us.*

They didn't thirst when he led them through the deserts; he caused the waters to flow out of the rock for them; he split the rock also, and the waters gushed out. (Isaiah 48:21)

CHAPTER THIRTEEN

Cleansing and Healing Stream 13

HEALING THROUGH THE PROPHETIC WORD

The Prophetic Word will bring healing, miracles, deliverance and wholeness. I am not talking about a so-called prophecy spoken from a knowledge of the Word out of a person's soulish realm, which is presumption, but rather a true prophetic Word filled with the Spirit and life—one directly from God. When God gives a word of knowledge, word of wisdom or a prophetic Word on healing, it becomes the *Rhema* that is filled with Spirit and life. The *Rhema* Word has within it, the spiritual seed that releases faith, life and power. Its fulfillment is accomplished through the operation of the Holy Spirit.

The Rhema Word has within it, the spiritual seed that releases faith, life and power.

Rhema is the Greek Word for the spoken Word of God. The Greek term for the written Word is *Logos*. The written "Word" in Hebrew is *memra*, a theological term the rabbis used before and after Jesus, when speaking of God's expression of Himself. . In the Jewish Targum, the Memra figures constantly as the manifestation of the divine power (Jewish Encyclopedia). When God inspires a prophetic Word, this *Rhema* carries with it, the power to produce the end result.

The Lord's will is clear on healing, and we preach and teach it from the Scriptures. A minister may believe strongly and speak from his/her faith using a scripture—this Word, if not prophetic, may miss the mark if not united with the sick one's faith. But when such a one receives a personal prophecy, a true prophetic Word from the Lord, it contains life-giving power to accomplish the miraculous.

A similarity exists between the Spirit of God quickening a biblical truth (preached or read) to you, which can happen frequently and become a Rhema to you, and a particular personal prophecy from the Lord. Thus, quoting the Word in preaching and teaching and communicating it to a particular person—but without the Spirit of God quickening it, can be different than receiving a download from God for a person or the Spirit of God directly, which is a *Rhema* word.

We see an example of a prophetic Word spoken to Naaman, a captain in the King of Aram's army. The prophet records:

> Then Elisha sent him a messenger, who said, "Go wash seven times in the Jordan and your flesh will be restored and you will be clean." (2 Kings 5:10 HCSB)

When Naaman did as Elisha instructed, the Word came to pass. In the New Testament, prophets are also active in speaking a *Rhema* and accomplishing healing—and this continues today. Jesus announced the Spirit of the Lord upon Him to proclaim good news to the poor, release to the captives, recovery of sight to the blind, to set at liberty the oppressed, and proclaim Jubilee (see Luke 4).

A boy whose family attended our church, which I knew personally over several years, suffered tremendously. I both observed this boy and fellowshipped with his parents. He could not participate in children's church. He would sometimes hide under a table, bite or kick the teacher, and demonstrate frustration. He bit a friend of mine who taught, and who continued to love him and exercise great patience with him. The experts diagnosed him with a disability that had to do with connecting what he heard and processing it.

This boy's parents stood in faith many years, spoke truth over him, and dealt with all the issues surrounding his care and education with much grace. I personally observed his mother tearing his food into little pieces for him when most children his age would have been able to handle their meals on their own.

A prophet, who ministered in our church sometimes annually, spoke a prophetic Word over this boy—to the extent that God was connecting something in his brain that needed rewiring. Oh, if you could see this young man today! God made him whole through the prophet's ministry. He is a miracle-child, handsome, articulate, smart and well behaved.

Something similar happened in my ministry during a healing meeting. A boy in our church had a learning difficulty, and an issue related to it—a repetitive and involuntary movement of his hands. Interestingly, but so like God, this boy's name often came up in prayer when he was very young—and again as he began school. His mother believed that if I prayed for him, he would be healed. Without going into great detail, she spoke this word over him, to me and to her husband. The day came for her to bring him forward for prayer, and God healed him. He is doing well in school, and the other issue has subsided as well. I believe her faith and the power of the prophetic word were at work, as well as the anointing.

We can prosper from the Word of God through a prophet. King Jehoshaphat proclaimed:

> Put your trust in the LORD your God and you will be established. Put your trust in His prophets and succeed." (2 Chronicles 20:20b)

A Rhema Through the Spirit of Counsel

It has happened that as the Spirit of Counsel comes upon me, and God speaks a Word of deliverance prophetically for someone through me, inner healing begins to manifest in the person. The prophetic Word acts as a surgeon's knife, cutting through to the root of the problem. Whether the person has a physical symptom, or an emotional symptom, God is able to bring change through "a Word to the weary in due season." We are an extension of the Lord's ministry on earth, and Isaiah prophesied of the Messiah:

> The Lord GOD has given Me the tongue of those who are instructed to know how to sustain the weary with a word. He awakens *Me* each morning; He awakens My ear to listen like those being instructed. (Isaiah 50:4 MSG)

Releasing Faith based on the Preaching and Teaching of the Word

The prophetic flow of the Word that brings healing and miracles is an avenue that is available through the ministry of the prophet, or a prophetic Word from God spoken as a Word of Wisdom or Knowledge. But the Word of God, united with faith in the hearer— believed and acted upon, can bring results when a person releases their faith, just as can a manifestation of the gifts of the Spirit.

This frequently happens in my ministry as people receive healing in their chairs. Sometimes this amounts to the Spirit of God quickening the *Logos* and it becomes a *Rhema* to the person, or the ministry of the Spirit resting on a person brings the healing. God alone knows the difference.

Often a person with a ministry to multitudes observes this type of healing manifestation. The minister may then ask any that were healed as the Word was proclaimed and the anointing released to come forward to testify. To God be the glory.

CHAPTER FOURTEEN

Healing Stream 14

THE POWER IN THE NAME OF JESUS

God speaks through Jeremiah: "Is not My word like fire?" declares the LORD, "and like a hammer which shatters a rock?" (Jeremiah 23:29). I love this verse. It emphasizes the power of the Word of God. It can consume like fire, and it can either destroy or build up like a hammer. The Word can have a pounding affect on any situation. With the Word, you can curse a cancer, disease or even a situation. God can tear down kingdoms with a Word. One Word from God sets nations to seek Him.

God created by speaking the Word, and He brought judgment through the Word spoken by His prophets. Jesus Christ is the Word manifested. John writes,

> In the beginning was the Word, and the Word was with God, and the Word was God. The same was in the beginning with God. All things were made by him; and without him was not anything made that was made. (John 1:1-3)

We see confirmation from these verses that Jesus is the Word of God. In the book of Revelation, He is also called "The Word of God." John records the heavenly vision, "And He is clothed with a robe dipped in blood; and His name is called The Word of God" (Revelation 19:13). This same chapter goes on to record other exalting titles: "And on His robe and on His thigh He has a name written, "KING OF KINGS AND LORD OF LORDS" (Revelation 19:16). Glory to His Name!

In an earlier chapter on confessing the Word, I explained that God and His Word are One. His Word is a part of Himself. God is One. You cannot separate Him from His Word. Jesus and His name are One, and the name is the Person and represents authority.

Similarly, you cannot be separated from your word. It reveals who you are. Just as your word and the keeping of such identify your character, the character of God and Jesus Christ are behind the Word of God.

As the Word of God, Jesus only spoke the Word of the Father. The Word of God is "God breathed", so when you read or speak the Word, you are speaking words backed up by the character of God.

The Amplified Bible adds a parenthetical phrase after speaking in the name of Jesus, "My Father will grant you all that you ask in My Name (as presenting all that I AM)" (John 16:24). This is speaking of the Person of Jesus—all that He is. God has vested authority and power in the name of Jesus—"all authority in heaven and on earth" (Matthew 28:19). You might think of it as the power of the Word, the power of the blood, and the power demonstrated at the resurrection. In the last day, with His resurrection power, He will raise us up with Him. When you pray or speak in the name of Jesus, you are speaking in His authority. Jesus explains:

> For this is the will of My Father, that everyone who beholds the Son and believes in Him will have eternal life, and I Myself will raise him up on the last day. (John 6:40)

An alternative translation says of the authority He gave believers,

> Jesus came and told his disciples, "I have been given all authority in heaven and on earth. Therefore, go and make disciples of all the nations, baptizing them in the name of the Father and the Son and the Holy Spirit." (Matthew 28:18-19 NLT)

Jesus indicates that God gave Him this authority upon the resurrection; however, we see that He already had authority that He demonstrated over demons, the elements, and sickness, even death. This new authority, all authority or complete authority, God gave Him for the Church, which is His body on earth. Jesus then gave the church this authority, the power of attorney to use His name so that He could fulfill His promise, "Whatever you ask in my name, that will I do that the Father may be glorified in the Son" (John 14:13). Remember, "ask" is used in the sense of "demand," as in oneness with Him; we speak for Him and require something to line up with our words.

I said earlier that healing and authority in the name of Jesus did not go away with the last of the apostles—the Apostle Christ Jesus is still alive—He has risen:

> Wherefore, holy brethren, partakers of the heavenly calling, consider the Apostle and High Priest of our profession, Christ Jesus. (Hebrews 3:1)

This living Savior never changes. The write of Hebrews says of Him, "Jesus Christ the same yesterday, and today, and forever" (Hebrews 13:8). Jesus Christ is still alive and is the same today as He was yesterday and yes, forever. He is still healing countless numbers today through His body, the Church.

The early believers used The Name, preached in The Name and healed in The Name. They were warned by the Sanhedrin not to preach or teach or do anything in That Name, but they could not (see Acts 4:17, 5:28). All they did, they did in the Name. They understood the power and authority in the name of Jesus. They used The Name as a shield and as a hammer, a battering ram for the purpose of the Good News.

The name of Jesus is synonymous with authority. The name represents the person, and authority. Jesus said, "Until now, you have asked nothing in My name; ask, and you will receive that your joy may be made full" (John 16:24). Our prayers to God are through Jesus, in His name, because He is our Covenant head, our Apostle and High Priest, and "He ever lives to make intercession for us" (Hebrews 7:25).

Through the name of Jesus, healing is available by all the cleansing and healing streams. We have authority and power as believers in the name of Jesus for healing the sick and casting out demons, in fact, all that Jesus said we would do.

Paul writing to the Corinthians asked this question: "Examine yourself to see if you are in the faith" (2 Corinthians 13:5). When you believe you are in danger or under attack. What name do you speak as a shield and a defense? Is it not the wonderful name of Jesus? Is this not The Name that causes demons to tremble and flee? Yes, and moreover, it is the name God exalted above all names: Paul extols:

> Wherefore God also hath highly exalted him, and given him a name which is above every name: That at the name of Jesus every knee should bow, of [things] in heaven, and [things] in earth, and [things] under the earth; And [that] every tongue should confess that Jesus Christ [is] Lord, to the glory of God the Father. (Philippians 2:9-11)

God gave Jesus authority and power on Earth. When He raised Jesus from the dead, He gave Him authority and power in Heaven and Earth, and under the Earth. He has authority in all three dimensions— and we are in His body and given His name to use.

Jesus tells us that some may use His name, yet not be under His authority. He said,

> Many will say to Me on that day; "Lord, Lord, did we not prophesy in Your name, and in Your name cast out demons, and in Your name perform many miracles?" (Matthew 7:22-23)

This is remarkable. The name of Jesus is so powerful that even those, who do not know the Lord in the truest sense, use His name to perform miracles, cast out demons, and prophesy. To know the Lord means to know Him experientially, as in a love relationship. While this verse has application to obedience, see that God has vested great authority and power in the name of Jesus. These people the Master refers to had faith in the Name and the Word's power and authority, but no love of The Name. John writes, "This is eternal life, that they may know You, the only true God, and Jesus Christ whom You sent." (John 17:3).

Faith in The Name is absolute trust and self-abandonment to the Person, power and Word of Jesus Christ.

What is faith in The Name? Faith in The Name is absolute trust and self-abandonment to the Person, power and Word of Jesus Christ. When you feel that you have tried and have exhausted all the streams of healing, and are struggling to know the Lord's leading for healing, just say The Name. Below are important pointers on the name of Jesus Christ:

Twelve Things You Should Know About the Name of Jesus

1. Salvation is only in the Name of Jesus. He is the Christ. Peter and Paul respectively exclaim,

> And there is salvation in no one else; for there is no other name under heaven given among men, by which we must be saved. (Acts 4:12)

> That if you confess with your mouth Jesus as Lord, and believe in your heart that God raised Him from the dead, you shall be saved. (Romans 10:9)

2. Eternal life is through His name. John writes,

> But as many as received Him, to them He gave the right to become children of God, even to those who believe in His name. But these have been written that you may believe that Jesus is the Christ, the Son of God; and that believing you may have life in His Name. (John 1:12, 20:31)

3. Signs and wonders follow The Name. Jesus says to us,

> And these signs will accompany those who have believed in My Name . . . they will cast out demons, they will lay hands on the sick and they will recover . . . (Mark 16:17-18)

3. Healing is in The Name, and we are to do His works in The Name. Jesus explains:

> Truly, truly, I say to you, he who believes in Me, the Works that I do shall he do also; and greater works than

these shall he do; because I go to the Father and whatever you ask in My name, that will I do, that the Father may be glorified in the Son. If you ask Me anything in My name, I will do it. (John 14:12-14)

When we do His works, we are to speak in His Name (demand, ask). God has vested power in the name of Jesus. We are not demanding that God do anything. That would be foolish. He already has done all. We are making a demand on the provision in The Name by using our delegated authority, the power of attorney He gave us of His name. With regard to sickness; for example, we would say, "In the name of Jesus, be healed." We have just asked in His name as regarding doing the greater works that He said we would do. We are using the authority in His name by commanding healing to come forth.

4. Believers are to pray to the Father in The Name. Jesus said, "Until now you have asked for nothing in My name; ask, and you will receive that your joy may be made full" (John 16: 24). This is an example of when we have a request of the Father, not one of delegated authority as with number 3 above.

5. When we believe and confess Jesus as Lord, we belong to God and He knows us—we bear His name. Paul writing to Timothy encouraged him in the faith:

> Nevertheless, the firm foundation of God stands, having this seal, "The Lord knows those who are His," and, "Everyone who names the name of the Lord is to abstain from wickedness." (2 Timothy 2:19)

> "I am the good shepherd, and I know My own and My own know Me." (John 10:14)

We are to speak and understand that in Christ, we bear His name. To bear His name means that wherever we go, His name is spoken by us to others. The Lord speaks of Paul and his mission,

But the Lord said to him, "Go, for he is a chosen instrument of Mine, to bear My name before the Gentiles and kings and the sons of Israel." (Acts 9:15)

6. God highly exalted Him and bestowed on Him the Name which is above every name, (see Philippians 2:9). He is seated at God's right hand in the place of honor. Hebrews says,

When He had made purification of sins, he sat down at the right hand of the Majesty on high; having become as much better than the angels, as He has inherited a more excellent name than they. (Hebrews 1:3)

Paul continues with this theme:

Which he brought about in Christ when He raised Him from the dead, and seated Him at His right hand in the heavenly places, far above all rule and authority and power and dominion, and every name that is named not only in this age but also in the one to come. (Ephesians 1:21)

We see that God made Jesus to be supreme in every way. Paul wrote a letter to the church showing Christ's supremacy. Writes Paul,

He is also the head of the body, the church; and He is the beginning, the first-born from the dead; so that he Himself might come to have first place in everything. (Colossians 1:16)

7. Whatever believers do is to be done in The Name, even service to others, and not just miracles. Paul explains,

And whatever you do in word or deed, do all in the name of the Lord Jesus, giving thanks through Him to God the Father. Whatever you do, do your work heartily, as for the Lord knowing that from the Lord

you will receive the reward of the inheritance. It is the
Lord Christ whom you serve. (Colossians 3:16, 23-24)

8. When you receive someone sent in His name, you receive Him and
the Father. His ministers are gifts to the Body of Christ. Jesus
said,

He who receives you receives Me, and he who receives
Me receives Him who sent Me. (Matthew 10:40)

9. When we use His name, we do it in Him, from under His authority
and in His kingdom. God removed us from the authority and
power of the enemy, and darkness, and put us into the new
kingdom, into its authority and power.

For He delivered us out of the control and dominion of
darkness, and transferred us to the kingdom of His
beloved Son. (Colossians 1:12)

10. Demons tremble at the name of Jesus. He took back our lost
authority. This becomes real to you only as you use the name of
Jesus. God made it all possible through Christ:

When He had disarmed the rulers and authorities, He
made a public display of them having triumphed over
them through Him. (Colossians 2:15)

You believe that God is One. You do well; the demons
also believe and shudder. (James 2:19)

11. You will be hated and persecuted for His name. Jesus says with
love in His voice:

Remember the word that I said to you, "A slave is not
greater than his master." If they persecuted Me, they
will also persecute you. (John 15:20)

Jesus also said that you are blessed when you are persecuted and slandered because of His name (see Matthew 5:10). I have come to believe that the word "blessed" has to do with our oneness with God. It is an experience and life that is marked by joy, even bliss, peace that cannot be shaken, and a love of God that gives us possession of His power. Paul writes to those in Rome, "The kingdom of God is righteousness, peace and joy in the Holy Spirit" (Romans 14:17).

The name "Jesus" is the English translation of the Hebrew name "Yeshua." It means "God is Salvation." God knew what He was doing when He to call His name Jesus. From now on, when you speak or whisper the name of Jesus, think Salvation. This Salvation lives in me. Yeshua HaMaschiach—Jesus Christ.

We could say many other things about The Name. But then as John says,

> If they should all be recorded, I suppose the world itself could not contain the books that would be written. (John 21:25)

Lord, I love Your Name.

They didn't thirst when he led them through the deserts; he caused the waters to flow out of the rock for them; he split the rock also, and the waters gushed out. (Isaiah 48:21)

CONCLUSION

Jesus took the stripes on His back and the wounds on His body so we could be whole. He came into this world to defeat the enemy and regain our dominion. John explains,

> The devil has sinned from the beginning. The Son of God appeared for this purpose, that He might destroy the works of the devil. (I John 3:8)

The devil may succeed in putting sickness on a Christian, but he cannot keep it on a Christian who knows who Christ is in Him—the Greater One. Through faith in His redemptive work and union with Him, we can testify to partaking of the righteousness of God. The devil is rendered powerless when we understand this. Paul tells the believers at Colossi,

> When He had disarmed the rulers and authorities, He made a public display of them, having triumphed over them through Him. (Colossians 2:15)

Since Jesus Christ has overcome Satan, and we are in Jesus, we share in His victory. Our union with Him, and authority in His name, means the devil is a defeated foe for us as well. We have many references that point to the entry of sin and sickness in the world, and many that tell us that we have authority over it through Jesus. The Apostle Peter said, "How God anointed Jesus of Nazareth with the Holy Spirit and with power, and He went about doing good, and healing all who were oppressed by the devil; for God was with Him" (Acts 10:38). God is with us—Emmanu'El.

A curse of sickness cannot stay on a Christian—one made righteous by the blood of Christ. Since we are redeemed from the curse, we can refuse to take or keep one.

> Like a sparrow in its flitting, like a swallow in its flying, so a curse without cause does not alight. (Proverbs 26:2)

A curse cannot stick to a person with the anointing of the Anointed One (Messiah). It cannot find a cause for one made righteous.

As Christians, we were never subject to the entire law of the Old Testament (see Acts 15). The ordinances were for the people of the law. We are under grace (see Romans 6:14). But the same principle of the law holds true, we are under a moral law—our righteousness in Christ does not exempt us from moral obligations.

Deuteronomy 28 speaks of blessings and curses. Having entered through the fall of man in the garden, sickness is now a curse and codified in the law. Christ redeemed us from the curse of the law (Galatians 3:13). This means we are redeemed from sickness and disease. We are redeemed from sin, sickness, lack and spiritual death into a resurrection life that includes life, health, safety and prosperity.

The totality of salvation, including healing, belongs to you, so do not allow sin or sickness to have dominion over you. Use any one of these healing streams, or combine them. The point is: be healed. Of all the examples given, the three streams of healing that are always available to you are Prayer, Communion, Praise and Worship, and Confession of the Word. The Word of God is important to all three. I admonish you as did Paul the Colossians: "Let the Word of Christ dwell richly in you" (Colossians 3:16). I remind you that the Word of God will have effect, and perform its work in you who believe (see 1 Thessalonians 2:13).

Why Are Some Not Healed So Easily?

Often those of us in healing ministries see so many wonderful healings and miracles that we have to guard against making healing sound so easy—when the experience of many is just the opposite. Some may have received ministry from well-known healing evangelists, received prayer in the local church, and read and studied to no end. I have a word for you. Stand.

I cannot explain why it takes a long season for some to be healed, or why some are not healed. While I believe they could be, and should be, they are not. The Bible says,

The secret things belong to the LORD our God, but the things revealed belong to us and to our sons forever, that we may observe all the words of this law. (Deuteronomy 29:29)

Only God can see the heart of those who so desire healing, and yet miss out. I encourage you; if you fall into this category, stand. Be sure your heart is free of any condemnation—especially repent of any lack of forgiveness and forgive. I once ministered to a man over a period of several months. During this time, he assured me that he saw himself righteous in Christ, that he had no unforgiveness in his heart, and did all that he knew to do to be healed, and in his case, survive. Yet, in private, to another he admitted to needing to see a miracle to believe in one. Sadly, on his deathbed he confessed a sin that weighed him down. If we have condemnation in our hearts, then our faith will just not work. I pray you take this incident to heart. I like to tell people, "If you have any kind of an internal ping or sense of tension when you think about anyone—take care of it."

If we have condemnation in our hearts, then our faith will just not work.

I have seen others who did not receive healing and desperately sought it from many sources. Some never release their faith with words or actions. I cannot tell you with absolute confidence what blocked their healing. Unbelief, lack of knowledge and faith, and disobedience are primary reasons many are blocked. I cannot say anyone who failed to be healed lacked faith. That is up to God. I will say that sometimes it is because "the secret things belong to the Lord."

God is not glorified in sickness! Just the opposite, He demonstrates His glory in miracles. I also do not believe it is His will for people to be sick. Again, God's will is just the opposite. It would be a sin to see a doctor if we truly believed it was God's will for us to be sick!

I love to see those to whom I minister receive miracles. It is humbling to know God will use such frail vessels to accomplish His will. I have been in healing lines myself, and can testify, that on occasion, I did not see a healing manifest. But I can also testify that on occasion, I have! Those who minister in healing have an anointing to minister to others, but must pursue their own healing like any other believer. I can testify that it is not always as easy as we show it could be and should be, but God is faithful. Sometimes God will use a doctor for helping the body mend, yet sometimes doctors can offer no hope. I say with you as does Paul,

> Therefore, take up the full armor of God, so that you will be able to resist in the evil day, and **having done everything, to stand firm.** (Ephesians 6:13 emphasis added)

A NOTE ON JOB'S BOILS AND PAUL'S THORNS

The devil has many scalps and hides from these two subjects. People will take a position about healing based on Job's boils and Paul's thorns! They challenge divine healing and seem to "know" more negative than God's redemption and healing through the stripes of Jesus, and they put more faith in what they have heard than in God's word.

The early church read Job at Passion Week, and they saw the parallels in Job's suffering and Christ's. Job was the most righteous man on earth in his day, and Christ in His days on Earth. Of course Christ was totally sinless.

I totally disagree with most who currently teach that Job opened a door for Satan through fear, and that Paul had an infirmity. No, God said Job was upright. They miss the point of Job's and Paul's suffering. As I was reading the book of Job one day, after having read it many times in several translations, I believe God began to show me a piece of the overall picture. Job only suffered less than a year and lived a long, long time. God healed Job and gave him double blessings. As I was reading Job, I began to say, "Ecclesiastes." This happened several times. We can hear from the Holy Spirit in different ways. I sometimes speak things out by the Spirit.

People seem to know more about Job's boils and Paul's thorns than God's redemption and healing through the stripes of Jesus, and they put more faith in what they have heard about them.

Thus, having read Job, read about Job, heard about Job, and preached about Job—incorrectly I might add, I went to the book of

Ecclesiastes. There I saw many parallels to Job in Ecclesiastes. Solomon provides many of the same conclusions in this book as appears in Job.

Solomon came to some very grand conclusions: Chiefly, you cannot always figure out God! Good things happen to evil people and bad things happen to good people. This conclusion amounted to Job's entire problem. He could not understand why God had not kept him safe from evil. He had enjoyed God's goodness and lived a good life. He has two chapters on his righteous deeds. Over and over, God says Job was righteous.

It is easy to miss the point of Job and Paul's suffering. It is more about your response when you do not understand why something is bad is occurring. Job stayed on God's side for many chapters, and then he lost it. He finally had it with his so-called friends and lack of immediate answers from God. He lost his children, livelihood, health, and worst of all, a wife who turned on him and said that he should curse God and die! No wonder Job cries, "Even if He kills me, I will hope in Him. I will still defend my ways before Him" (Job 13:15). Job is saying, "I did no sin to bring this terrible thing on me. I think this is all from God. Everything is gone but my life, and even if He now takes that, I will trust—put my hope in Him. And I will not admit to sin I did not commit."

What is the answer to the book of Job, and to suffering that you do not understand? You cannot figure out God. Jesus said it this way, "He rains on the just and the unjust—the righteous and the unrighteous" (see Matthew 5:45). Solomon concluded in essence: Enjoy life, fear God and keep his commandments. Live eternally minded.

What was God's purpose in allowing Job to suffer—seems to me it is so he can prove Job would remain in faith, stand, and then bring him closer. Sometimes we do not go "all out for God" until we have to cleave to Him with every ounce of our strength. With Paul, the afflictions caused him to draw on more grace, move closer to the Lord. Again, the point is what we do in the midst of trials, when we suffer and when we don't understand. Will we rejoice and trust God to use our obedience for a redemptive purpose? Paul responds,

You're looking at this backwards. The issue in Jerusalem is not what they do to me, whether arrest or murder, but what the Master Jesus does through my obedience. Can't you see that? (Acts 21:13b MSG)

The devil wants to distort the Word, just like Job's friends kept accusing him of sin, and Job didn't believe he had sinned. If Job had sinned and opened a door through fear, God would have not called him upright. God is on our side. He does not look for an opportunity to send calamity if we mess up.

People often go inward, checking themselves for sin, when they get sick—no, stand on the word and get rid of it. God is not putting sickness on people, or sending demons to them. The Old Testament writers had little to say about Satan—other than in the book of Job. They viewed everything as from God. Jesus shows us that Satan is the oppressor, and God is the Healer. I totally disagree with those who would say God puts it on you or sends you a devil. If someone says they heard God say that He sent it, then I question whether they heard from God.

We live in a fallen world, and we experience some sickness from that reason alone. We also disobey and bring on sickness through our actions—like overeating and getting diabetes. The devil didn't bring that type of diabetes, we did.

I see people healed of all kinds of sicknesses—spiritual, physical and emotional. Many times, God is so merciful. Recently, I saw my father-in-law healed of paralysis from a stroke as I prayed for him. Cancers have disappeared. In some cases, we stand longer, but I do know pain cannot stay in Jesus' presence. God is so merciful that he placed the gifts of the Spirit in the body to see His body healed.

Do people have to repent to be healed? The question should be; "Why would they not want to repent regardless? I do not believe healing is a bartering chip with God. The Word says.

He fulfilled Isaiah's well-known sermon: He took our illnesses, He carried our diseases. (Matthew 8:17 MSG)

But it was our sins that did that to him, that ripped and tore and crushed him—our sins! He took the

punishment, and that made us whole. Through his
bruises we get healed. (Isaiah 53:5 MSG)

Jesus Christ suffered the chastening for our peace, our
wholeness. We respond in love and live a holy life because we are
redeemed—and stay free. When we do not understand why we suffer,
or loved ones suffer, stay on God' side. Trust Him.
I chose to have the word "TRUST" placed on a wall in my
secret place. The letters are large gold letters, reminding me that "faith
is more precious than gold, though tested by fire."

Pure gold put in the fire comes out of it proved pure;
genuine faith put through this suffering comes out
proved genuine. When Jesus wraps this all up, it's your
faith, not your gold, that God will have on display as
evidence of his victory. (1Peter 1:7 MSG)

Lord, I trust You.

They didn't thirst when he led them through the deserts; he caused the waters to flow out of the rock for them; he split the rock also, and the waters gushed out. (Isaiah 48:21)

BIBLIOGRAPHY

Kenyon, E. W., <u>Jesus the Healer.</u> Kenyon's Gospel Publishing Society, P.O Box 973, Lynnwood, WA 98046-0973, 1977. www.kenyons.org. Used by Permission.

Christian, Dr. Shirley, <u>Types and Shadows, Prophetic Pictures of Wholeness in Christ</u>. Xulon Press: 2006. Used by permission.

Unless otherwise indicated, all scripture is from the <u>New American Standard Bible</u>, copyright 1960, 1962, 1963, 1968, 1971,1972, 1973, 1975, 1977, 1995 by th3 Lockman Foundation, Used by Permission.

<u>New International Version</u> (NIV). Copyright © 1973, 1978, 1984 by <u>International Bible Society.</u> Used by Permission.

Peterson, Eugene. <u>Message Bible (MSG)</u>. Navpress: Copyright © 1993, 1994, 1995, 1996, 2000, 2001, 2002. Used by permission.

<u>New Living Translation</u> (NLT) Holy Bible. Copyright © 1996, 2004 by Tyndale Charitable Trust. Used by permission of Tyndale House Publishers. Used by Permission.

Green, Jay P. <u>Modern King James Version </u>(MKJV). Copyright © 1962.

Scriptures marked as HCSB are taken from the <u>Holman Christian Standard Bible</u>. Nashville, Tennesee: Holman Bible Publishers, 2000.

Stern, David. <u>Jewish New Testament</u> (JNT): Jewish New Testament Publications, Inc , Clarksville, Maryland, 1979. Used by permission.

Strong, James. <u>Strong's Exhaustive Concordance of the Bible</u>. World Bible Publishers, Inc., 1986.

If you are not confident about your eternal home, or have any doubt as to your peace with God, then pray this prayer out loud:

Father,

I repent of my sins, and I ask you to forgive me and cleanse me by the blood of Jesus Christ. Your Word says that *if I confess with my mouth Jesus as Lord, and believe in my heart that God raised Him from the dead, I will be saved*, according to Romans 10:9. I believe Jesus died for me and rose from the dead. Though the blood of Jesus, I believe I am free, according to Ephesians 1:7. I believe I have eternal life according to John 3:16, and that I do not come into judgment, but out of death into life, according to John 5:24. Please confirm your love to me now by giving me supernatural love, joy, and peace. I pray in Jesus name. Amen.

ABOUT THE AUTHOR

Dr. Shirley Christian actively fulfills a role of instruction and oversight as Professor of Biblical Studies at a Bible Institute in Lubbock, Texas. Her many years of ministry in a healing school with the gifts of the Spirit in operation, and the things she had gone through personally, worked a deep compassion within her for the lost and hurting. The Holy Spirit entrusted Shirley with a strong intercessory prayer life, healing and prophetic giftings, and through her brings truth and deliverance to the Body of Christ. Shirley flows in streams of His grace, streams of intercession, cleansing, healing and revelation.

The Holy Spirit inspired the motto, Streams of His Grace, for Shirley Christian Ministries during a time of prayer. Shirley believes the inspiration for the motto is based on how the Holy Spirit manifests His presence in streams of revelation, power and intercession.

If you enjoyed Cleansing and Healing Streams by Dr. Shirley Christian, please visit the ministry website for other products and books such as Types and Shadows, Prophetic Pictures of Wholeness in Christ, and Living the Fasted Life. You will also find free downloads of teaching and confession CDS on her ministry website:

www.shirleychristian.org

www.ingramcontent.com/pod-product-compliance
Lightning Source LLC
LaVergne TN
LVHW011356080426
835511LV00005B/317